100
MINCE
Dishes

100 MINCE *Dishes*

Edited by
Stella Joyce

CHANCELLOR
PRESS

Contents

NOTES

Standard spoon measurements are used in all recipes
1 tablespoon = one 15 ml spoon
1 teaspoon = one 5 ml spoon
All spoon measurements are level.
Where amounts of salt and pepper are unspecified in recipes the cook should use her discretion. Canned foods are used with their juices unless otherwise specified.
Ovens and grills (broilers) should be preheated to the specified temperature or heat setting. For all recipes, quantities are given in metric, imperial and American measures. Follow one set of measures only, because they are not interchangeable.

First published in Great Britain in 1984

This edition published in 1994 by Chancellor Press
an imprint of Reed Consumer Books Limited
Michelin House, 81 Fulham Road, London SW3 6RB
and Auckland, Melbourne, Singapore and Toronto

Copyright © Reed International Books Limited 1984

ISBN 1 85152 474 6

A CIP catalogue record for this book is available from
the British Library

Printed in Hong Kong

Frontispiece: Chilli Con Carne (page 8)
(Photograph: New Zealand Lamb Information Bureau)

Introduction

For many of us, mince means shepherd's pie – the remains of the Sunday joint, minced with the old hand mincer clamped to the kitchen table, mixed with leftover gravy and topped with mashed potato. It was nourishing and economical but hardly exciting.

Others may remember it from student days, when it was the cheapest meat it was possible to buy and we somehow made half a pound feed four hungry friends!

Today all meat is much more expensive and mince has ceased to be a cheap standby. We need to find more interesting and exciting ways of cooking it, and fortunately there is no shortage of recipes. Almost every country has a favourite mince dish, from Mexican chilli to Greek moussaka, from German meatballs to Italian lasagne.

Different varieties of mince are also becoming freely available. Pork and veal mince are now easy to find, which makes it possible for us to vary traditional dishes as well as experiment with new ones. If you have any difficulty finding the right sort of mince, ask your butcher to prepare it for you.

As food processors become more common, it is also possible to make your own mince.

Although, strictly speaking, a processor chops food, the result is very similar and you can vary the texture as required – fairly coarse for a meaty casserole, very fine for firm, smooth-textured meatballs or pâtés.

Whether you buy the mince or prepare your own, it is still economical, not only because it uses a less expensive cut of meat, but also because there is no waste – no fat to cut off, no gristle to discard. For the same reasons it is popular with children who can be finicky eaters. It also lends itself to being stretched – with kidney beans in a chilli con carne, with

pasta in lasagne or with vegetables, as in Cornish pasties. If you have an extra guest for supper you can usually add a little more to a mince dish to make it go further.

Remember when buying mince that it can go off more quickly than meat in the piece, so always buy it fresh and use it as soon as possible. Beef, lamb and pork mince contain quite a lot of fat, so it is often possible to cook them without additional fat. Place the meat in a saucepan over a low heat until the fat begins to run, then raise the heat and fry more briskly. Minced veal is lean and should be fried with a little additional fat.

A mince dish is often soft in texture, so it is a good idea to combine it with a crisp-textured food as a contrast. Try placing slices of French bread spread with garlic or herb butter on top of a casserole for the last 15 minutes of the cooking time. A crumbly pie crust is equally successful or accompany a pasta dish with a crisp green salad or coleslaw.

Mince happily absorbs many different flavourings. Herbs, spices, wine, lemon rind and cheese all blend beautifully with different types of mince, and there can be few combinations that have not been tried somewhere in the world. The recipes in this book cover a wide range of dishes, flavours and eating situations. They can be very simple, such as hamburgers – if you've never made your own, do try them. They are far superior to commercial ones, with a delicious flavour and meaty texture, and you can add your own favourite seasonings. There are simple family meals, such as pies and casseroles, picnic and summer foods, which can be eaten cold, or more exotic international dishes suitable for entertaining. In short, mince is economical, adaptable, versatile and, if you follow the recipes in this book, delicious!

International Flavours

Mexican Tacos

METRIC/IMPERIAL

2 tablespoons
  vegetable oil
1 onion, chopped
1 teaspoon chilli
  powder
1 teaspoon salt
350 g/12 oz minced
  beef
1 × 227 g/8 oz can
  tomatoes
1 × 65 g/2½ oz can
  tomato purée
1 tablespoon lemon
  juice
8 taco shells
50 g/2 oz Cheddar
  cheese, grated
1 red pepper, cored,
  seeded and cut in
  rings

AMERICAN

2 tablespoons
  vegetable oil
1 onion, chopped
1 teaspoon chili
  powder
1 teaspoon salt
¾ lb ground beef
1 × 8 oz can tomatoes
¼ cup tomato paste
1 tablespoon lemon
  juice
8 taco shells
½ cup shredded
  Cheddar cheese
1 red pepper, cored,
  seeded and cut into
  rings

Heat the oil in a large frying pan (skillet) and gently sauté the onion until soft. Add the chilli powder and salt, fry for 2 minutes, then add the meat and fry, stirring, until evenly browned. Drain off any surplus fat and add the tomatoes, tomato purée (paste) and lemon juice. Cover and simmer gently for 30 minutes.

Arrange the taco shells open side up on a serving dish and fill with the beef mixture. Sprinkle the cheese over the meat and top with the pepper rings.
Serves 4

Moussaka

METRIC/IMPERIAL

4 tablespoons oil
2 onions, finely
  chopped
350 g/12 oz minced
  beef or lamb
1 tomato, peeled and
  chopped
1 bay leaf
pinch of dried thyme
salt
freshly ground black
  pepper
300 ml/½ pint tomato
  juice
1 large aubergine,
  sliced
1 egg
150 ml/¼ pint single
  cream

AMERICAN

¼ cup oil
2 onions, finely
  chopped
¾ lb ground beef or
  lamb
1 tomato, peeled and
  chopped
1 bay leaf
pinch of dried thyme
salt
freshly ground black
  pepper
1¼ cups tomato juice
1 large eggplant,
  sliced
1 egg
⅔ cup light cream

Heat half the oil in a saucepan and sauté the onions for 2 to 3 minutes. Add the meat and continue cooking until well browned. Stir in the tomato, bay leaf, thyme and salt and pepper, then pour on the tomato juice. Stir well. Bring to the boil, reduce heat and simmer for 10 minutes. Meanwhile fry the aubergine (eggplant) slices in the remaining oil.

Layer the aubergine (eggplant) slices with the meat mixture in an ovenproof dish. Beat the egg and cream together and pour over the top. Bake in a preheated moderate oven (180°C/ 350°F, Gas Mark 4) for 35 to 40 minutes, until topping is set. When serving remove bay leaf.
Serves 4

Mexican Tacos

Boston Bean Casserole

METRIC/IMPERIAL	AMERICAN
1 kg/2 lb minced beef	2 lb ground beef
1 beef stock cube	2 beef bouillon cubes
225 g/8 oz carrots, finely diced	½ lb carrots, finely diced
2 × 447 g/15¾ oz cans baked beans	2 × 16 oz cans baked beans
2 tablespoons maple syrup	2 tablespoons maple syrup
salt	salt
freshly ground black pepper	freshly ground black pepper

In a large non-stick saucepan, gently fry the meat, stirring, until browned. Crumble in the stock cube (bouillon cubes), add the carrots and continue cooking gently for 5 minutes.

Stir in the beans and maple syrup. Add salt and pepper to taste, then cover and simmer very gently for 1 hour.

Serves 6 to 8

Minced Beef Pizzaiola

METRIC/IMPERIAL	AMERICAN
2 tablespoons oil	2 tablespoons oil
2 large onions, chopped	2 large onions, chopped
2 cloves garlic, crushed	2 cloves garlic, crushed
½ teaspoon dried oregano	½ teaspoon dried oregano
575 g/1¼ lb minced beef	1¼ lb ground beef
1 × 298 g/10½ oz can condensed tomato soup	1 × 10½ oz can condensed tomato soup
2–3 tablespoons red wine or sherry	2–3 tablespoons red wine or sherry
To Serve:	**To Serve:**
225–350 g/8–12 oz spaghetti	2–3 cups spaghetti

Heat the oil in a large saucepan and sauté the onions and garlic until golden. Add the oregano and the meat and continue cooking, stirring, until meat has browned. Lower heat and simmer for 30 minutes, stirring occasionally. Add the tomato soup, wine or sherry and mix well. Simmer for a further 10 minutes.

To serve, cook the pasta, arrange on a serving plate and top with the meat mixture.

Serves 4

Chilli Con Carne

METRIC/IMPERIAL	AMERICAN
250 g/8 oz red kidney beans, soaked overnight	¾ cup red kidney beans, soaked overnight
2 tablespoons oil	2 tablespoons oil
2 medium onions, chopped	2 medium onions, chopped
450 g/1 lb minced beef	1 lb ground beef
1–2 teaspoons chilli powder	1–2 teaspoons chili powder
2 tablespoons tomato purée	2 tablespoons tomato paste
300 ml/½ pint beef stock	1¼ cups beef stock
1 × 397 g/14 oz can tomatoes	1 × 14 oz can tomatoes

Drain beans, place in a saucepan and cover with water. Bring to the boil and allow to boil for 10 minutes. Drain. Heat the oil in a large saucepan and sauté the onions until soft. Add the meat and continue cooking, stirring, until well browned. Stir in the chilli powder, tomato purée (paste), stock and canned tomatoes. Add the drained beans and bring to the boil. Reduce heat, cover and simmer for 1 to 1½ hours.

Serves 4

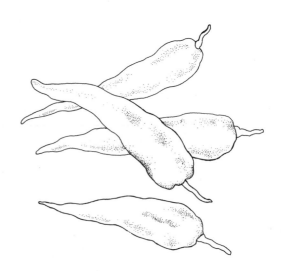

Pork and Cheese Jalousie

METRIC/IMPERIAL	AMERICAN
225 g/8 oz minced pork	½ lb ground pork
1 small onion, chopped	1 small onion, chopped
1 teaspoon dried oregano	1 teaspoon dried oregano
grated rind of ½ lemon	grated rind of ½ lemon
salt	salt
freshly ground black pepper	freshly ground black pepper
1 × 342 g/12 oz packet frozen puff pastry, thawed	1 × ¾ lb packet frozen puff paste, thawed
50 g/2 oz Swiss cheese, sliced	½ cup sliced Swiss cheese
2 tomatoes, sliced	2 tomatoes, sliced
beaten egg or milk to glaze	beaten egg or milk to glaze

Mix together the meat, onion, oregano, lemon rind, and salt and pepper. Roll out the pastry (dough) to a rectangle 30 cm × 25 cm/12 inches × 10 inches and cut into two lengthwise, having one piece slightly larger than the other.

Place the smaller piece of pastry (dough) on a baking sheet and arrange the meat mixture on it to come within 2.5 cm/1 inch of the edges. Place the cheese on top and cover with the tomatoes.

Fold the remaining piece of pastry lengthwise and make cuts from the folded edge, 1 cm/½ inch apart, to within 2.5 cm/1 inch of the opposite edge. Unfold the pastry and place carefully over the other piece, sealing the edges well. Brush with egg or milk, and bake in a preheated moderately hot oven (200°C/400°F, Gas Mark 6) for 30 to 40 minutes until risen and golden.
Serves 4 to 6

Spiced Lamb Terrine

METRIC/IMPERIAL	AMERICAN
150 ml/¼ pint light stock	⅔ cup light stock
15 g/½ oz gelatine	½ oz/2 envelopes unflavored gelatin
450 g/1 lb cooked lamb, minced	1 lb cooked lamb, ground
50 g/2 oz cooked ham, chopped	¼ cup chopped cooked ham
25 g/1 oz fresh brown breadcrumbs	½ cup soft brown bread crumbs
1 teaspoon curry powder	1 teaspoon curry powder
¼ teaspoon chilli powder	¼ teaspoon chili powder
1 tablespoon mango chutney	1 tablespoon mango chutney
1 teaspoon lemon juice	1 teaspoon lemon juice
salt	salt

Place the stock in a small bowl and sprinkle on the gelatine. Allow to soak for a few minutes, then stand the basin in a pan of hot water until melted.

Place all the other ingredients in a bowl and mix well together, adding salt to taste. Pour on the gelatine mixture and stir well.

Press into a 450 g/1 lb loaf tin (7 × 3 inch loaf pan) and refrigerate until firm. To serve, dip the tin (pan) in hot water and turn out.
Serves 4

Spiced Beef Hash

METRIC/IMPERIAL	AMERICAN
1 tablespoon oil	1 tablespoon oil
1 onion, chopped	1 onion, chopped
450 g/1 lb minced beef	1 lb ground beef
1 teaspoon mixed spice	1 teaspoon ground allspice
2 tablespoons vinegar	2 tablespoons vinegar
150 ml/¼ pint water	⅔ cup water
1 × 298 g/10½ oz can condensed oxtail soup	1 × 10½ oz can condensed oxtail soup
2–4 sticks celery, chopped	2–4 stalks celery, chopped
2 pickled cucumbers, chopped	2 dill pickles, chopped
100 g/4 oz rice, cooked	1 cup rice, cooked

Heat the oil in a saucepan, add the onion and meat, and sauté for 10 to 15 minutes, stirring occasionally. Add the spice, vinegar and water, and simmer for 40 minutes. Add remaining ingredients and reheat adding a little more water if needed.
Serves 4

Chinese Savoury Mince with Green Peppers

METRIC/IMPERIAL	AMERICAN
2 tablespoons oil	2 tablespoons oil
450 g/1 lb minced beef	1 lb ground beef
2 tablespoons chopped onion	2 tablespoons chopped onion
½ green pepper, cored, seeded and diced	½ green pepper, cored, seeded and diced
1 × 326 g/11½ oz can sweetcorn	1 × 11½ oz can whole kernel corn
1 × 227 g/8 oz can tomatoes	1 × 8 oz can tomatoes
1 beef stock cube	2 beef bouillon cubes
300 ml/½ pint water	1¼ cups water
salt	salt
freshly ground black pepper	freshly ground black pepper

Heat the oil in a saucepan and fry the meat lightly for 5 minutes. Drain off excess fat and add the vegetables. Crumble in the stock cube, add the water and bring to the boil, stirring. Cover and simmer gently for 50 minutes. Add salt and pepper to taste. Serve with cooked rice.
Serves 4 to 6

Bacon and Veal Paupiettes

METRIC/IMPERIAL	AMERICAN
1 egg white	1 egg white
450 g/1 lb minced veal	1 lb ground veal
100 g/4 oz fresh white breadcrumbs	2 cups soft white bread crumbs
grated rind of 1 lemon	grated rind of 1 lemon
4 tablespoons chopped fresh herbs	¼ cup chopped fresh herbs
salt	salt
freshly ground black pepper	freshly ground black pepper
8 large rashers back bacon	8 large back bacon slices
Sauce:	**Sauce:**
2 tablespoons olive oil	2 tablespoons olive oil
25 g/1 oz butter	2 tablespoons butter
juice of 1 lemon	juice of 1 lemon
300 ml/½ pint chicken stock	1¼ cups chicken stock
1 teaspoon cornflour	1 teaspoon cornstarch
4 tablespoons single cream	¼ cup light cream
1 egg yolk	1 egg yolk
To garnish:	**To garnish:**
lemon wedges and fresh herbs	lemon wedges and fresh herbs

Whisk the egg white lightly with a fork, add the meat, breadcrumbs, lemon rind, herbs and salt and pepper, and mix well. Divide the mixture into 8 and roll into balls, then flatten each into a patty shape.

Wrap each patty in a rasher (slice) of bacon, securing with a cocktail stick (toothpick). Heat the oil and butter in a large, shallow pan and sauté the paupiettes for 2 to 3 minutes each side until golden.

Add the lemon juice and stock, cover and simmer for 15 to 20 minutes. With a slotted spoon, remove the paupiettes to a serving dish and keep warm. Mix the cornflour (cornstarch), cream and egg yolk together in a bowl and pour half the hot stock from the pan into the mixture. Stir well. Return the cornflour (cornstarch) mixture to the pan and heat very gently, stirring constantly, until a creamy sauce forms.

Remove cocktail sticks (toothpicks) from the paupiettes and pour over the sauce. Garnish with lemon wedges and fresh herbs.
Serves 4

Bacon and Veal Paupiettes
(Photograph: Pork Farms)

Indian Spiced Minced Beef

METRIC/IMPERIAL	AMERICAN
1 tablespoon oil	1 tablespoon oil
2 cloves garlic, crushed	2 cloves garlic, crushed
1 large onion, chopped	1 large onion, chopped
1 teaspoon Madras curry powder	1 teaspoon Madras curry powder
450 g/1 lb minced beef	1 lb ground beef
150 ml/¼ pint water	⅔ cup water
1 tablespoon sweet chutney	1 tablespoon sweet pickle relish
1 × 298 g/10½ oz can condensed vegetable soup	1 × 10½ oz can condensed vegetable soup
salt (optional)	salt (optional)

Heat the oil in a saucepan. Sauté the garlic and onion until golden. Add curry powder and fry for 1 to 2 minutes. Add the meat and fry, stirring frequently, until browned and partly cooked. Add the water, chutney (relish) and vegetable soup, mix well and bring to the boil. Reduce heat and simmer for 40 to 45 minutes. Add salt if required. Serve with boiled rice.
Serves 3 to 4

Beef Popovers

METRIC/IMPERIAL	AMERICAN
Batter:	**Batter:**
75 g/3 oz plain flour	¾ cup all-purpose flour
salt	salt
freshly ground black pepper	freshly ground black pepper
1 egg	1 egg
150 ml/¼ pint milk and water mixed	⅔ cup milk and water mixed
Filling:	**Filling:**
175 g/6 oz minced beef	¾ cup firmly packed ground beef
3 tablespoons flour	3 tablespoons flour
1 × 298 g/10½ oz can condensed oxtail soup	1 × 10½ oz can condensed oxtail soup
25 g/1 oz dripping	2 tablespoons drippings
½ soup can water	½ soup can water

For the batter, sift the flour, salt and pepper into a bowl. Break in the egg and add half the milk and water mixture. Beat together, gradually

incorporating the flour, to form a thick smooth batter. Add the rest of the milk and water mixture.

For the filling, mix together the meat, flour and half the oxtail soup. Divide the mixture into four and shape into balls. Place dripping in four 20 cm/4 inch Yorkshire pudding tins (popover pans) and heat in a preheated hot oven (220°C/425°F, Gas Mark 7) until just smoking. Divide the meatballs and the batter mix between the 4 tins and return to the oven for 20 to 25 minutes, until the batter is risen and golden. In a saucepan, heat the remaining soup with the water and serve as a sauce.
Serves 4

Mexican Mince

METRIC/IMPERIAL	AMERICAN
1 tablespoon oil	1 tablespoon oil
1 onion, chopped	1 onion, chopped
450 g/1 lb minced beef	1 lb ground beef
4 teaspoons chilli powder	4 teaspoons chili powder
1 × 142 g/5 oz can tomato purée	1 × 5 oz can tomato paste
2 teaspoons red wine vinegar	2 teaspoons red wine vinegar
salt	salt
freshly ground black pepper	freshly ground black pepper
1 green pepper, cored, seeded and chopped	1 green pepper, cored, seeded and chopped
225 g/8 oz frozen sweetcorn	1½ cups whole kernel corn

In a large saucepan heat the oil and sauté the onion until soft. Add the meat, chilli powder, tomato purée (paste), vinegar, salt and pepper. Stir well, cover and cook over a low heat for 30 minutes. Add the green pepper and cook for a further 30 minutes, stirring occasionally. Add the sweetcorn and cook for 5 minutes more. Serve with plain boiled rice.
Serves 4

Kofta Curry

METRIC/IMPERIAL	AMERICAN
225 g/8 oz minced lamb	½ lb ground lamb
1 small onion, finely chopped	1 small onion, finely chopped
2 cloves garlic, crushed	2 cloves garlic, crushed
1 teaspoon garam masala	1 teaspoon garam masala
salt	salt
freshly ground black pepper	freshly ground black pepper
1 egg, beaten	1 egg, beaten
oil for frying	oil for frying
1 × 283 g/10 oz can curry sauce	1 × 10 oz can curry sauce
a few mint leaves, roughly chopped, to garnish	a few mint leaves, roughly chopped, to garnish

Mix the meat, onion, garlic, spices and salt and pepper. Add the beaten egg and mix well. Shape into 8 to 10 meatballs. Fry in hot oil in a shallow pan on all sides until evenly browned. Drain well. In a large saucepan, heat the curry sauce and add the meatballs, cover and simmer for 15 minutes. Serve garnished with chopped mint leaves.
Serves 4

Hungarian Stuffed Peppers

METRIC/IMPERIAL	AMERICAN
4 large green peppers	4 large green peppers
1 large onion, chopped	1 large onion, chopped
450 g/1 lb minced beef	1 lb ground beef
1 × 50 g/2 oz packet goulash casserole mix	1 × 2 oz packet goulash casserole mix
150 ml/¼ pint water	⅔ cup water
1 × 227 g/8 oz can tomatoes	1 × ½ lb can tomatoes
1 × 198 g/7 oz can sweetcorn, drained	1 × 7 oz can whole kernel corn, drained
150 ml/¼ pint soured cream	⅔ cup sour cream

Cut the tops off the peppers and remove the seeds. Blanch the peppers and the tops in boiling salted water for 5 minutes, then drain upside down on kitchen paper. Put the onion and meat in a large frying pan (skillet) and cook without additional fat for 10 minutes, stirring, until meat is cooked. Blend the casserole mix with the water and canned tomatoes, add to the beef and cook, stirring, until thick. Add the corn, and divide the mixture between the peppers. Put the lid on each pepper and stand in an ovenproof dish containing a little water. Bake in a preheated moderately hot oven (190°C/375°F, Gas Mark 5) for about 20 minutes.

Heat the sour cream gently in a small saucepan and serve with the peppers.
Serves 4

Meatballs

Cheese Meatballs

METRIC/IMPERIAL	AMERICAN
25 g/1 oz margarine	2 tablespoons margarine
1 onion, chopped	1 onion, chopped
275 g/10 oz minced pork	$1\frac{1}{4}$ cups firmly packed ground pork
50 g/2 oz fresh breadcrumbs	1 cup soft bread crumbs
1 egg, beaten	1 egg, beaten
100 g/4 oz processed cheese spread	$\frac{3}{4}$ cup processed cheese spread
25 g/1 oz plain flour	$\frac{1}{4}$ cup all-purpose flour
salt	salt
freshly ground black pepper	freshly ground black pepper
2 tablespoons oil	2 tablespoons oil
To serve:	**To serve:**
200 g/7 oz long-grain rice	1 cup long-grain rice
1 × 198 g/7 oz can sweetcorn	1 × 7 oz can whole kernel corn

Melt the margarine in a saucepan and lightly sauté the onion until soft. Mix the meat, drained onion, breadcrumbs and egg.

Divide the cheese spread into 8 portions and roll each into a ball. Divide the meat mixture into 8 portions.

Sift flour and salt and pepper onto a plate. With floured hands, wrap a portion of meat mixture round each ball of cheese. Shape into balls and roll in seasoned flour.

Heat the oil in a frying pan (skillet) and gently fry the meatballs for 8 to 10 minutes, turning them occasionally. Meanwhile, boil the rice in a saucepan with salted water until tender, and heat the sweetcorn. Drain the rice, combine with the sweetcorn and place in a warm serving dish. Arrange the meatballs on top and serve.
Serves 4

Cheese Meatballs
(Photograph: Kraft Foods Ltd.)

Meatballs Napoletana

METRIC/IMPERIAL	AMERICAN
50 g/2 oz fresh breadcrumbs	1 cup soft bread crumbs
450 g/1 lb minced beef	1 lb ground beef
2 cloves garlic, crushed	2 cloves garlic, crushed
1 tablespoon chopped parsley	1 tablespoon chopped parsley
1 teaspoon lemon juice	1 teaspoon lemon juice
50 g/2 oz grated cheese	$\frac{1}{2}$ cup shredded cheese
pinch of mixed spice	pinch of ground allspice
salt	salt
freshly ground black pepper	freshly ground black pepper
2 eggs, beaten	2 eggs, beaten
To finish:	**To finish:**
25 g/1 oz plain flour	$\frac{1}{4}$ cup all-purpose flour
2 tablespoons oil	2 tablespoons oil
1 green pepper, cored, seeded and diced	1 green pepper, cored, seeded and diced
1 × 298 g/$10\frac{1}{2}$ oz can tomato spaghetti sauce	1 × $10\frac{1}{2}$ oz can tomato spaghetti sauce

Place all the meatball ingredients in a bowl and mix well together. Shape into small balls about 2.5 cm/1 inch in diameter and dust with flour. Fry the meatballs in the oil for about 5 minutes, turning occasionally until evenly browned. Drain on kitchen paper. Pour off most of the fat from the pan and sauté the green pepper in the remainder. Return the meatballs to the pan, add the spaghetti sauce and simmer for 20 minutes until the meatballs are cooked.
Serves 4

Ginger and Raisin Meatballs

METRIC/IMPERIAL	AMERICAN
750 g/1½ lb minced beef	1½ lb ground beef
1 egg, beaten	1 egg, beaten
100 g/4 oz fresh breadcrumbs	2 cups soft bread crumbs
25 g/1 oz wholewheat flour	¼ cup wholewheat flour
1 onion, finely chopped	1 onion, finely chopped
salt	salt
freshly ground black pepper	freshly ground black pepper
6 gingernut biscuits, crushed	6 gingersnaps, crushed
600 ml/1 pint beef stock	2½ cups beef stock
50 g/2 oz brown sugar	⅓ cup brown sugar
50 g/2 oz seedless raisins	⅓ cup seedless raisins
2 tablespoons lemon juice	2 tablespoons lemon juice

In a bowl, mix the meat with the egg, bread-crumbs, flour, onion and salt and pepper. Shape into small meatballs. Place the biscuits (cookies) in a saucepan, add the stock and bring to the boil. Stir in the sugar, raisins and lemon juice. Reduce heat, add the meatballs and cook gently for 30 minutes, stirring occasionally. Serve with pasta or rice.
Serves 6

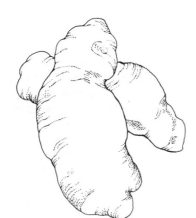

Party Porklets

METRIC/IMPERIAL	AMERICAN
1 large onion, finely chopped	1 large onion, finely chopped
450 g/1 lb minced pork	1 lb ground pork
225 g/8 oz pork and beef sausagemeat	½ lb pork and beef sausagemeat
1 × 99 g/3½ oz packet country stuffing mix	1 × 3 oz packet stuffing mix
1 egg, beaten	1 egg, beaten
1 tablespoon Tabasco sauce	1 tablespoon hot pepper sauce
salt	salt
freshly ground black pepper	freshly ground black pepper

Place all ingredients in a bowl and mix well together. Shape into small balls the size of a walnut. Place on a greased baking sheet and bake in a preheated moderately hot oven (200°C/400°F, Gas Mark 6) for 15 minutes. Spear with cocktail sticks (toothpicks) to serve.
Serves 6

Pork Meatballs in Mushroom Sauce

METRIC/IMPERIAL	AMERICAN
350 g/12 oz minced pork	¾ lb ground pork
50 g/2 oz white breadcrumbs	1 cup soft bread crumbs
1 egg, beaten	1 egg, beaten
salt	salt
freshly ground black pepper	freshly ground black pepper
½ teaspoon sage	½ teaspoon sage
grated rind of ½ lemon	grated rind of ½ lemon
25 g/1 oz butter	2 tablespoons butter
1 × 298 g/10½ oz can condensed mushroom soup	1 × 10½ oz can condensed mushroom soup
½ soup can milk	½ soup can milk

In a bowl, combine the pork, breadcrumbs, egg, salt and pepper, sage and lemon rind. Mix well and shape into about 16 balls.

Heat the butter in a frying pan (skillet) and gently fry the meatballs until golden. Add the condensed soup to the pan with the milk and stir in gently. Cover and simmer very gently for 25 to 30 minutes.
Serves 4

Chinese Meatballs with Sweet and Sour Sauce

METRIC/IMPERIAL	AMERICAN
Sauce:	**Sauce:**
1 × 340 g/12 oz can pineapple chunks	1 × 12 oz can pineapple chunks
1 medium carrot, cut into matchsticks	1 medium carrot, cut into matchsticks
½ green pepper, cored, seeded and cut into thin strips	½ green pepper, cored, seeded and cut into thin strips
1 stick celery, finely sliced	1 stalk celery, finely sliced
1 tablespoon olive oil	1 tablespoon olive oil
40 g/1½ oz cornflour	⅓ cup cornstarch
1 tablespoon soy sauce	1 tablespoon soy sauce
25 g/1 oz brown sugar	2 tablespoons brown sugar
1 beef stock cube	2 beef bouillon cubes
3 tablespoons vinegar	3 tablespoons vinegar
Meatballs:	**Meatballs:**
450 g/1 lb minced beef	1 lb ground beef
1 egg, beaten	1 egg, beaten
1 small onion, grated	1 small onion, grated
1 beef stock cube, crumbled	2 beef bouillon cubes, crumbled
salt	salt
freshly ground black pepper	freshly ground black pepper
Batter:	**Batter:**
50 g/2 oz plain flour	½ cup all-purpose flour
salt	salt
freshly ground black pepper	freshly ground black pepper
4 tablespoons water	4 tablespoons water
1 tablespoon oil	1 tablespoon oil
1 egg white	1 egg white
oil for frying	oil for frying

First make the sauce: Drain the juice from the can of pineapple and make it up to 450 ml/¾ pint (2 cups) with water. In a saucepan, sauté the carrot, pepper and celery in hot oil for 2 to 3 minutes, stirring constantly. In a bowl, blend the cornflour (cornstarch) with a little of the pineapple juice to form a smooth paste, then gradually stir in the remaining liquid. Add to the vegetables in the saucepan and bring to the boil, stirring, until the sauce is smooth and clear. Add the soy sauce, sugar, crumbled stock cube (bouillon cubes), vinegar and pineapple chunks. Keep warm while preparing the meatballs.

In a bowl, combine the meat, egg, onion, stock cube (bouillon cubes), salt and pepper and mix well. Shape the mixture into about 20 small balls. To make the batter, mix the flour, salt and pepper, water and oil until smooth. Whisk the egg white until stiff and fold into the batter.

Dip the meatballs in the batter and deep fry in hot oil for 5 or 6 minutes. Drain well and serve hot with the sauce.
Serves 4 to 6

Spicy Lamb Balls

METRIC/IMPERIAL	AMERICAN
450 g/1 lb lean minced lamb	1 lb lean ground lamb
1 small onion, finely chopped	1 small onion, finely chopped
1 egg, beaten	1 egg, beaten
1 tablespoon sultanas, chopped	1 tablespoon golden raisins, chopped
2 tablespoons finely chopped hazelnuts	2 tablespoons finely chopped hazelnuts
1–2 teaspoons ground allspice	1–2 teaspoons ground allspice
2 tablespoons chopped parsley	2 tablespoons chopped parsley
salt	salt
freshly ground black pepper	freshly ground black pepper
2 tablespoons oil	2 tablespoons oil

Place all the ingredients, except the oil, in a bowl, mix thoroughly and shape into small balls.

Heat the oil in a frying pan (skillet) and cook the meatballs gently, turning occasionally until they are golden brown and cooked through. Drain on kitchen paper towels. Serve with salad and chutney.
Serves 6 to 8

Curried Meatballs

METRIC/IMPERIAL	AMERICAN
1 egg, beaten	1 egg, beaten
salt	salt
freshly ground black pepper	freshly ground black pepper
$\frac{1}{2}$ teaspoon curry powder	$\frac{1}{2}$ teaspoon curry powder
1 teaspoon fennel seed	1 teaspoon fennel seed
25 g/1 oz fresh breadcrumbs	$\frac{1}{2}$ cup soft bread crumbs
1 small onion, grated	1 small onion, grated
450 g/1 lb minced beef	1 lb ground beef
Coating and sauce:	**Coating and sauce:**
4 tablespoons flour	4 tablespoons flour
2 tablespoons curry powder	2 tablespoons curry powder
2 tablespoons oil	2 tablespoons oil
300 ml/$\frac{1}{2}$ pint beef stock	$1\frac{1}{4}$ cups beef stock
1 tablespoon mango chutney	1 tablespoon mango chutney
2 teaspoons lemon juice	2 teaspoons lemon juice

In a large bowl mix the egg with the salt, pepper, curry powder and fennel seed. Add the breadcrumbs and onion and leave to stand for half an hour. Add breadcrumb mixture to the meat and mix well.

Form the mixture into 15 to 20 balls. Mix the flour and curry powder on a plate and coat the meatballs. Heat the oil in a large, shallow pan and sauté the meatballs gently for 10 to 15 minutes until well cooked. Remove with a slotted spoon and keep warm.

Add any remaining flour and curry powder mixture to the pan, mix well and stir in the stock, chutney and lemon juice. Bring to the boil, stirring until thickened. Pour over the meatballs and serve.

Serves 4

Middle Eastern Meatballs with Spiced Yogurt Sauce

METRIC/IMPERIAL	AMERICAN
Sauce:	**Sauce:**
150 g/5.2 oz plain yogurt	$\frac{2}{3}$ cup plain yogurt
1 teaspoon ground coriander	1 teaspoon ground coriander
1 teaspoon ground cumin	1 teaspoon ground cumin
$\frac{1}{4}$ teaspoon ground cinnamon	$\frac{1}{4}$ teaspoon ground cinnamon
1 teaspoon lemon juice	1 teaspoon lemon juice
Meatballs:	**Meatballs:**
1 egg, beaten	1 egg, beaten
1 tablespoon dried mint	1 tablespoon dried mint
1 tablespoon dried parsley	1 tablespoon dried parsley
350 g/12 oz minced beef	$\frac{3}{4}$ lb ground beef
350 g/12 oz minced lamb	$\frac{3}{4}$ lb ground lamb
1 tablespoon ground coriander	1 tablespoon ground coriander
salt	salt
freshly ground black pepper	freshly ground black pepper
oil for frying	oil for frying

First make the sauce: Mix all the ingredients together and leave to stand in the refrigerator for 1 hour. To make the meatballs, mix the egg with the mint and parsley in a small bowl and leave to stand for half an hour. Put the meats in a bowl and add the egg mixture, coriander and salt and pepper. Mix well. Shape into 16 balls. Heat the oil in a shallow pan and fry the meatballs gently, turning frequently, for 10 to 12 minutes, ensuring that they are well cooked. Serve with the chilled sauce.

Serves 4

Middle Eastern Meatballs with Spiced Yogurt Sauce (Photograph: McCormick Foods (UK) Ltd)

Pancakes, Pies & Pasties

Matador Pancakes

METRIC/IMPERIAL	AMERICAN
Pancakes:	**Pancakes:**
100 g/4 oz flour	1 cup flour
pinch of salt	pinch of salt
1 egg	1 egg
300 ml/½ pint milk	1¼ cups milk
Filling:	**Filling:**
1 × 411 g/14½ oz can minced steak	1 × 14½ oz can ground steak
1 onion, chopped	1 onion, chopped
100 g/4 oz mushrooms, sliced	1 cup sliced mushrooms
1 × 298 g/10½ oz can condensed tomato soup	1 × 10½ oz can condensed tomato soup
crushed crisps	crushed potato chips

To make the pancakes, sift the flour with the salt and beat in the egg and milk to give a smooth batter. Make 8 pancakes. Place the meat, onion and mushrooms in a saucepan and heat gently for 10 minutes.

Spread the meat mixture over the cooked pancakes, roll up and place in a shallow oven-proof dish. Pour over the soup and sprinkle with the crushed crisps (potato chips). Bake in a preheated moderately hot oven (190°C/375°F, Gas Mark 5) for 15 to 20 minutes.
Serves 4

Spicy Meat Plait

METRIC/IMPERIAL	AMERICAN
450 g/1 lb minced beef	1 lb ground beef
3 tablespoons parsley stuffing mix	3 tablespoons parsley stuffing mix
2 teaspoons mustard powder	2 teaspoons mustard powder
salt	salt
freshly ground black pepper	freshly ground black pepper
1 medium onion, chopped	1 medium onion, chopped
2 tablespoons tomato purée	2 tablespoons tomato paste
1 clove garlic, crushed	1 clove garlic, crushed
1 egg, beaten	1 egg, beaten
1 × 342 g/12 oz packet frozen shortcrust pastry, thawed	1 × ¾ lb package frozen basic pie dough, thawed

To make the filling, mix all the ingredients together, binding with half the egg.

Roll out the pastry (dough) to a rectangle 30 cm × 35 cm/12 inches × 14 inches and place on a baking sheet. Spoon the meat mixture down the centre of the pastry (dough), in a strip about 7.5 cm/3 inches wide and to within 5 cm/2 inches of each end. Cut off the corners and make a series of diagonal cuts down each side to within 2.5 cm/1 inch of the filling. Brush edges with water, fold in the ends, then bring the sides up to cover the meat, overlapping the strips to give a plaited (braided) effect. Brush with the remaining beaten egg and bake in a preheated moderately hot oven (200°C/400°F, Gas Mark 6) for 15 minutes. Reduce heat to 190°C/375°F, Gas Mark 5, and cook for a further 25 minutes. Serve hot or cold.
Serves 4 to 6

Matador Pancakes
(Photograph: John West Foods)

Creamy Veal and Egg Pie

METRIC/IMPERIAL	AMERICAN
25 g/1 oz butter	2 tablespoons butter
450 g/1 lb minced veal	1 lb ground veal
3 spring onions, chopped	3 scallions, chopped
50 g/2 oz mushrooms, chopped	$\frac{1}{2}$ cup chopped mushrooms
1 × 397 g/14 oz packet frozen puff pastry, thawed	1 × 14 oz packet frozen puff paste, thawed
beaten egg to glaze	beaten egg to glaze
Sauce:	**Sauce:**
40 g/1$\frac{1}{2}$ oz butter	$\frac{1}{3}$ cup butter
40 g/1$\frac{1}{2}$ oz flour	$\frac{1}{3}$ cup flour
300 ml/$\frac{1}{2}$ pint milk	1$\frac{1}{4}$ cups milk
2 eggs, hard-boiled and chopped	2 eggs, hard-cooked and chopped
salt	salt
freshly ground black pepper	freshly ground black pepper

Melt the butter in a saucepan and fry the meat gently until just cooked. Place in a bowl and stir in the spring onions (scallions) and mushrooms.

For the sauce, melt the butter in a saucepan and add the flour. Cook for 1 minute. Gradually stir in the milk. Bring to the boil, stirring, until thickened. Add the eggs and veal mixture. Add salt and pepper. Remove from heat and allow to cool. Roll out the pastry to a 25 cm/10 inch square and place on a baking sheet. Place the filling on the pastry in a diamond shape. Damp the edges of the pastry and bring the four corners up to meet in the centre. Seal the edges well and crimp. Brush with beaten egg and bake in a preheated moderately hot oven (200°C/400°F, Gas Mark 6) for 30 to 35 minutes, until well risen and golden.
Serves 4 to 6

Spring Rolls

METRIC/IMPERIAL	AMERICAN
1 tablespoon oil	1 tablespoon oil
3 spring onions, chopped	3 scallions, chopped
1 stick celery, chopped	1 stalk celery, chopped
50 g/2 oz minced pork	$\frac{1}{4}$ cup ground pork
50 g/2 oz cooked prawns	$\frac{1}{3}$ cup shelled shrimp, cooked
3 canned water chestnuts, chopped	3 canned water chestnuts, chopped
50 g/2 oz bean sprouts	1 cup bean sprouts
75 g/3 oz cooked long-grain rice (25 g/1 oz uncooked)	$\frac{1}{2}$ cup cooked long-grain rice (2 tablespoons uncooked)
2 teaspoons cornflour	2 teaspoons cornstarch
2 teaspoons soy sauce	2 teaspoons soy sauce
1 tablespoon sherry	1 tablespoon sherry
8 ready made pancakes, cooked on one side only (see page 23)	8 ready made pancakes, cooked on one side only (see page 23)
1 egg, beaten	1 egg, beaten

Heat the oil in a saucepan and sauté the onions (scallions) and celery until soft. Add the meat, prawns (shrimp), water chestnuts, bean sprouts and rice, and sauté lightly until meat is well browned. Blend cornflour (cornstarch) with the soy sauce and sherry. Add to the pan and cook until the sauce has thickened, stirring all the time. Remove from heat. Spoon equal quantities of the filling in the centre of each pancake, on the cooked side. Brush the edges with beaten egg. Fold in the sides and roll up to make a neat parcel. Seal all the edges with egg. Leave in a cool place for 10 minutes to set.

Heat deep fat to 190°C/375°F, and fry the rolls two at a time, until crisp and golden. Drain well and serve hot.
Makes 8 spring rolls

Spring Rolls
(Photograph: US Rice Council)

Pasta Dishes

Lasagne

METRIC/IMPERIAL	AMERICAN
175 g/6 oz quick cooking lasagne	6 oz quick cooking lasagne noodles
50 g/2 oz grated Parmesan cheese	$\frac{1}{2}$ cup grated Parmesan cheese
Meat sauce:	**Meat sauce:**
2 tablespoons oil	2 tablespoons oil
1 onion, chopped	1 onion, chopped
450 g/1 lb minced beef	1 lb ground beef
1 × 397 g/14 oz can tomatoes	1 × 14 oz can tomatoes
2 tablespoons Worcestershire sauce	2 tablespoons Worcestershire sauce
1 tablespoon tomato purée	1 tablespoon tomato paste
1 teaspoon mixed herbs	1 teaspoon mixed herbs
150 ml/$\frac{1}{4}$ pint beef stock	$\frac{2}{3}$ cup beef stock
salt	salt
freshly ground black pepper	freshly ground black pepper
White sauce:	**White sauce:**
40 g/1$\frac{1}{2}$ oz butter	$\frac{2}{3}$ cup butter
40 g/1$\frac{1}{2}$ oz plain flour	$\frac{2}{3}$ cup all-purpose flour
600 ml/1 pint milk	2$\frac{1}{2}$ cups milk

To make the meat sauce, heat the oil in a saucepan and sauté the onion until soft. Add the meat and fry until browned. Stir in the remaining ingredients. Adjust the seasoning, cover and simmer for 20 minutes, stirring occasionally. For the white sauce, melt the butter in a saucepan, add the flour and cook for 1 minute. Remove from the heat and gradually add the milk. Return to the heat and bring to the boil, stirring, until thickened. Add salt and pepper to taste.

Grease a shallow oblong or square dish and line with half the lasagne. Cover with half the meat sauce and half the white sauce. Repeat the layers then top with the cheese.

Bake in a preheated moderate oven (180°C/350°F, Gas Mark 4) for 45 minutes.
Serves 6

Lasagne
(Photograph: Pasta Information Service)

Pork and Pasta Hotpot

METRIC/IMPERIAL	AMERICAN
2 large onions, sliced	2 large onions, sliced
4 tablespoons English mustard	4 tablespoons English mustard
1 tablespoon vinegar	1 tablespoon vinegar
3 tablespoons treacle	3 tablespoons molasses
75 g/3 oz brown sugar	$\frac{1}{2}$ cup brown sugar
2 tablespoons Worcestershire sauce	2 tablespoons Worcestershire sauce
300 ml/$\frac{1}{2}$ pint chicken stock	1$\frac{1}{4}$ cups chicken stock
1 × 397 g/14 oz can tomatoes	1 × 14 oz can tomatoes
450 g/1 lb minced pork	1 lb ground pork
3 tablespoons tomato purée	3 tablespoons tomato paste
1 teaspoon salt	1 teaspoon salt
350 g/12 oz pasta wheels	3 cups pasta wheels

Place the onions, mustard, vinegar, treacle (molasses), sugar, Worcestershire sauce, stock and tomatoes in a large saucepan. Bring to the boil, reduce heat and simmer gently for 5 minutes. Add the meat, tomato purée (paste) and salt, cover and continue cooking for a further 30 minutes. Stir in the pasta wheels, and simmer for 12 minutes adding a little boiling water if mixture becomes dry.
Serves 4 to 6

Quick Pasta Gratin

METRIC/IMPERIAL	AMERICAN
15 g/½ oz butter	1 tablespoon butter
1 medium onion, finely chopped	1 medium onion, finely chopped
1 medium carrot, grated	1 medium carrot, grated
350 g/12 oz minced veal	¾ lb ground veal
1 tablespoon plain flour	1 tablespoon all-purpose flour
1 teaspoon dried oregano	1 teaspoon dried oregano
1 tablespoon tomato purée	1 tablespoon tomato paste
1 × 397 g/14 oz can tomatoes	1 × 14 oz can tomatoes
100 g/4 oz button mushrooms, sliced	1 cup sliced button mushrooms
300 ml/½ pint chicken stock	1¼ cups chicken stock
salt	salt
freshly ground black pepper	freshly ground black pepper
175 g/6 oz pasta shapes	1½ cups pasta shapes
Cheese sauce:	**Cheese sauce:**
25 g/1 oz butter	2 tablespoons butter
25 g/1 oz plain flour	¼ cup all-purpose flour
300 ml/½ pint milk	1¼ cups milk
salt	salt
freshly ground black pepper	freshly ground black pepper
175 g/6 oz Edam cheese, grated	1½ cups shredded Edam cheese

Melt the butter in a large frying pan (skillet) and sauté the onion and carrot for 5 minutes. Stir in the veal and cook, stirring until lightly browned. Sprinkle in the flour and oregano and cook for 2 minutes. Stir in the tomato purée (paste), tomatoes, mushrooms and stock. Bring to the boil, stirring, and season with salt and pepper. Reduce heat and simmer for 5 minutes.

To make the sauce, melt the butter in a saucepan, add the flour and cook for 1 minute. Remove from the heat and gradually stir in the milk. Return to the heat and bring to the boil, stirring until thickened. Continue cooking for 2 minutes, remove from the heat, season to taste and add 100 g/4 oz (1 cup) of the cheese. Cook the pasta shapes in boiling salted water until tender; drain.

To assemble the dish, place half the meat mixture in a shallow ovenproof dish and scatter over half the pasta. Pour over remaining meat mixture and top with remaining pasta. Pour over the cheese sauce and sprinkle on the remaining cheese.

Bake in a preheated moderate oven (180°C/350°F, Gas Mark 4) for 30 to 35 minutes, until golden.
Serves 4

Minced Beef and Pasta Casserole

METRIC/IMPERIAL	AMERICAN
25 g/1 oz lard or margarine	2 tablespoons shortening or margarine
1 onion, chopped	1 onion, chopped
1 clove garlic, crushed	1 clove garlic, crushed
450 g/1 lb minced beef	1 lb ground beef
300 ml/½ pint beef stock	1¼ cups beef stock
1 × 227 g/8 oz can tomatoes	1 × 8 oz can tomatoes
1 × 219 g/7¾ oz can baked beans	1 × 8 oz can baked beans
½ teaspoon dried mixed herbs	½ teaspoon dried mixed herbs
2 teaspoons paprika	2 teaspoons mild paprika
2 teaspoons Worcestershire sauce	2 teaspoons Worcestershire sauce
75 g/3 oz pasta whirls or shells	¾ cup pasta whirls or shells
salt	salt
freshly ground black pepper	freshly ground black pepper
fresh chopped parsley to garnish	fresh chopped parsley to garnish

Heat the lard (shortening) or margarine in a saucepan and gently sauté the onion and garlic until soft. Add the meat and cook over a high heat until browned, stirring. Add the remaining ingredients except for the parsley. Bring to the boil and cover. Reduce heat and simmer gently for 45 minutes, until meat is tender and pasta cooked. Serve sprinkled with a little chopped parsley.
Serves 6

Minced Beef and Pasta Casserole

Pasta Leek Savoury

METRIC/IMPERIAL
2 medium leeks,
  sliced
175 g/6 oz noodles or
  pasta rings
150 ml/¼ pint water
225 g/8 oz minced
  pork
100 g/4 oz
  mushrooms,
  chopped
1 tablespoon oil
salt
freshly ground black
  pepper
150 g/6 oz grated
  cheese
600 ml/1 pint hot
  white sauce (see
  page 31)

AMERICAN
2 medium leeks,
  sliced
1½ cups noodles or
  pasta rings
⅔ cup water
½ lb ground pork
1 cup chopped
  mushrooms
1 tablespoon oil
salt
freshly ground black
  pepper
1½ cups shredded
  cheese
2½ cups hot white
  sauce (see page 31)

Place half the leeks in a casserole. Add half the dry pasta and pour over the water.

In a shallow pan, fry the meat and mushrooms in the oil until lightly browned, season with the salt and pepper and add to the casserole. Top with remaining leeks and pasta.

Stir 100 g/4 oz (1 cup) cheese into the hot white sauce. Spread over the casserole. Sprinkle with the remaining cheese. Bake in a preheated moderate oven (180°C/350°F, Gas Mark 4) for 45 minutes.
Serves 3 to 4

Mexican Spaghetti Supper

METRIC/IMPERIAL
1 large onion, finely
  chopped
4 tablespoons oil
450 g/1 lb minced beef
2 teaspoons chilli
  powder
salt
freshly ground black
  pepper
1 large green pepper,
  cored, seeded and
  chopped or cut in
  strips
150 ml/¼ pint beef
  stock
1 × 425 g/15 oz can
  spaghetti in tomato
  sauce
3 tablespoons soured
  cream (optional)

AMERICAN
1 large onion, finely
  chopped
¼ cup oil
1 lb ground beef
2 teaspoons chili
  powder
salt
freshly ground black
  pepper
1 large green pepper,
  cored, seeded and
  chopped or cut in
  strips
⅔ cup beef stock
1 × 15 oz can
  spaghetti in tomato
  sauce
3 tablespoons sour
  cream (optional)

Sauté the onion gently in the oil for 3 minutes in a large, shallow frying pan (skillet). Add the meat and cook until lightly browned. Add the chilli powder according to taste. Add salt and pepper to taste. Stir in the green pepper and stock, cover and cook gently for 20 minutes. Add the canned spaghetti and heat through, stirring. Swirl sour cream over the top if liked.
Serves 4

Spaghetti Bolognese

METRIC/IMPERIAL	AMERICAN
Bolognese sauce:	**Bolognese sauce:**
2 tablespoons oil	2 tablespoons oil
1 onion, chopped	1 onion, chopped
1 clove garlic, crushed	1 clove garlic, crushed
450 g/1 lb minced beef	1 lb ground beef
150 ml/$\frac{1}{4}$ pint red wine (optional)	$\frac{2}{3}$ cup red wine (optional)
$\frac{1}{2}$ teaspoon mixed herbs	$\frac{1}{2}$ teaspoon mixed herbs
1 × 397 g/14 oz can tomatoes	1 × 14 oz can tomatoes
2 tablespoons tomato purée	2 tablespoons tomato paste
450 ml/$\frac{3}{4}$ pint beef stock	2 cups beef stock
salt	salt
freshly ground black pepper	freshly ground black pepper
To serve:	**To serve:**
225 g/$\frac{1}{2}$ lb spaghetti	$\frac{1}{2}$ lb spaghetti
25 g/1 oz butter	2 tablespoons butter
50 g/2 oz grated Parmesan cheese	$\frac{1}{2}$ cup grated Parmesan cheese

Heat the oil in a saucepan and sauté the onion and garlic until golden. Add the meat and cook, stirring, until well browned. Add the wine if used, then stir in the herbs, tomatoes, tomato purée (paste) and stock. Bring to the boil and add salt and pepper to taste. Reduce heat and simmer for 45 minutes, stirring occasionally.

Meanwhile, cook the spaghetti in boiling salted water until just tender. Drain and add the butter, stirring until melted. Arrange around the edge of a heated serving dish, pour the meat sauce into the centre and sprinkle with Parmesan.
Serves 4

Sweet and Sour Pork with Peaches

METRIC/IMPERIAL	AMERICAN
450 g/1 lb minced pork	1 lb ground pork
100 g/4 oz fresh white breadcrumbs	2 cups soft white bread crumbs
2 tablespoons soy sauce	2 tablespoons soy sauce
3 tablespoons chopped parsley	3 tablespoons chopped parsley
salt	salt
freshly ground black pepper	freshly ground black pepper
1 egg, beaten	1 egg, beaten
1 tablespoon cornflour	1 tablespoon cornstarch
3 tablespoons oil	3 tablespoons oil
4 sticks celery, cut in 5 cm/2 inch pieces	4 stalks celery, cut in 2 inch pieces
3 onions, quartered	3 onions, quartered
1 × 411 g/14$\frac{1}{2}$ oz can peach slices, drained	1 × 14 oz can peach slices, drained
150 ml/$\frac{1}{4}$ pint chicken stock	$\frac{2}{3}$ cup chicken stock
2 tablespoons white wine vinegar	2 tablespoons white wine vinegar
350 g/12 oz pasta twists	3 cups pasta twists
1 red pepper, cored, seeded and cut in strips to garnish	1 red pepper, cored, seeded and cut in strips to garnish

Mix together the meat, breadcrumbs, soy sauce, parsley, salt and pepper, and egg, and shape into 16 patties. Coat with the cornflour (cornstarch), and brown in the oil in a shallow flameproof casserole. Remove the patties with a slotted spoon and fry the celery and onions in the remaining oil until lightly browned. Return the patties to the casserole. Add the peaches, stock and vinegar. Bring to the boil, cover and transfer to a preheated moderate oven (180°C/ 350°F, Gas Mark 4) for 1 hour.

Cook the pasta twists in boiling salted water until tender. Drain and place on a warmed serving dish. Arrange the pork and peach mixture on top and garnish with red pepper.
Serves 4 to 6

Vegetables with Mince

Veal-Stuffed Cucumbers

METRIC/IMPERIAL	AMERICAN
4 small cucumbers (about 450 g/1 lb total)	4 small cucumbers (about 1 lb total)
2 onions, chopped	2 onions, chopped
25 g/1 oz butter or margarine	2 tablespoons butter or margarine
450 g/1 lb minced veal	1 lb ground veal
salt	salt
freshly ground black pepper	freshly ground black pepper
1 tablespoon chopped parsley	1 tablespoon chopped parsley
100 g/4 oz cooked rice	1 cup cooked rice
600 ml/1 pint chicken stock	2½ cups chicken stock
75 g/3 oz grated cheese	¾ cup shredded cheese

Peel the cucumbers, cut in half lengthwise and remove the seeds. In a saucepan, sauté the onions in the butter or margarine until golden brown. Add the meat, salt, pepper and parsley. Allow to brown well then stir in the rice. Mix well and use to fill the cucumber shells. Place in a shallow ovenproof dish, pour over the stock and bake in a preheated moderately hot oven (200°C/400°F, Gas Mark 6) for 15 minutes. Sprinkle the cheese over and cook for 10 minutes more.
Serves 4

Beef and Cabbage Pie

METRIC/IMPERIAL	AMERICAN
1 spring cabbage	1 spring cabbage
25 g/1 oz butter	2 tablespoons butter
5 processed cheese slices	5 processed cheese slices
450 g/1 lb minced beef	1 lb ground beef
25 g/1 oz fresh white breadcrumbs	½ cup soft white bread crumbs
½ teaspoon ground nutmeg	½ teaspoon ground nutmeg
½ teaspoon ground cinnamon	½ teaspoon ground cinnamon
salt	salt
freshly ground black pepper	freshly ground black pepper
1 egg, beaten	1 egg, beaten

Separate all the large leaves from the cabbage and blanch in boiling salted water for 5 minutes. Drain.

Melt the butter in a small saucepan and use to grease a 20 cm/8 inch shallow cake tin (pan). Line the base and sides with cabbage leaves, having the stalks at the outer edges. Press down well and cover with a layer of cheese slices.

Mix the meat with the breadcrumbs, spices and salt and pepper, and bind with the egg. Place in the lined tin and smooth the surface.

Cover with foil, place in a roasting tin (pan) and add boiling water to come halfway up the side of the cake tin (pan). Bake in a preheated moderately hot oven (200°C/400°F, Gas Mark 6) for 1 to 1¼ hours. Turn out and cut into wedges to serve.
Serves 4

Veal-Stuffed Cucumbers
(Photograph: US Rice Council)

Stuffed Onions with Sweet and Sour Sauce

METRIC/IMPERIAL	AMERICAN
4 large onions	4 large onions
Stuffing:	**Stuffing:**
225 g/8 oz minced pork	$\frac{1}{2}$ lb ground pork
100 g/4 oz bran cereal	1 cup bran cereal
1 medium cooking apple, peeled, cored and chopped	1 large tart apple, peeled, cored and chopped
50 g/2 oz blanched almonds, chopped	$\frac{1}{2}$ cup chopped almonds
1 teaspoon dried mixed herbs	1 teaspoon dried mixed herbs
1 egg, beaten	1 egg, beaten
salt	salt
freshly ground black pepper	freshly ground black pepper
Sauce:	**Sauce:**
4 tablespoons clear honey	4 tablespoons clear honey
4 tablespoons malt vinegar	4 tablespoons malt vinegar
2 tablespoons soy sauce	2 tablespoons soy sauce
3 tablespoons tomato purée	3 tablespoons tomato paste
1 tablespoon dried mixed herbs	1 tablespoon dried mixed herbs
2 cloves garlic, crushed	2 cloves garlic, crushed
1 teaspoon ground ginger	1 teaspoon ground ginger
2 tablespoons water	2 tablespoons water

Remove the skin from the onions and cut off the roots. Blanch in boiling water for 10 minutes. Drain and leave until cool enough to handle. Scoop the flesh out of the centres with a teaspoon, leaving 2 to 3 layers to form a firm shell. Chop the scooped-out flesh and place it in a saucepan with the meat. Cook over a low heat without additional fat until meat is cooked. Add the cereal, apple, almonds and herbs and cook for a further 2 minutes. Remove from the heat and mix in the egg and salt and pepper. Spoon the stuffing into the onions, heaping it up if necessary. Place them in an ovenproof dish, just large enough to hold them closely. Mix all the sauce ingredients together and bring to the boil. Pour over the onions. Bake in a preheated moderately hot oven (190°C/375°F, Gas Mark 5) for 30 to 35 minutes until onions are cooked.
Serves 4

Stuffed Vine Leaves with Egg and Lemon Sauce

METRIC/IMPERIAL	AMERICAN
25–30 vine leaves, fresh or canned	25–30 vine leaves, fresh or canned
1 tablespoon olive oil	1 tablespoon olive oil
1 onion, chopped	1 onion, chopped
175 g/6 oz minced lamb	$\frac{3}{4}$ cup firmly packed ground lamb
1 teaspoon dried mint	1 teaspoon dried mint
1 tablespoon chopped parsley	1 tablespoon chopped parsley
salt	salt
freshly ground black pepper	freshly ground black pepper
$\frac{1}{2}$ teaspoon mixed spice	$\frac{1}{2}$ teaspoon ground allspice
50 g/2 oz cooked rice	$\frac{1}{2}$ cup cooked rice
juice of $\frac{1}{2}$ lemon	juice of $\frac{1}{2}$ lemon
chicken stock (see method)	chicken stock (see method)
Sauce:	**Sauce:**
25 g/1 oz butter	2 tablespoons butter
1 tablespoon flour	1 tablespoon flour
200 ml/$\frac{1}{3}$ pint chicken stock	$\frac{7}{8}$ cup chicken stock
1 egg	1 egg
juice of $\frac{1}{2}$ lemon	juice of $\frac{1}{2}$ lemon

If using fresh vine leaves, blanch for a few minutes in boiling salted water. For canned leaves, rinse thoroughly with cold water. Drain. Heat the oil in a saucepan and sauté the onion until soft. Add the meat and cook gently until browned. Add the herbs, salt and pepper, spice and rice. Mix well. Put a teaspoonful of the mixture on each vine leaf. Fold in the sides of each leaf and roll up tightly to make small parcels.

Pack the stuffed leaves close together in the base of a saucepan, making two layers if necessary. Pour over the lemon juice and enough stock to come halfway up the leaves. Cover the pan and simmer very gently for about 40 minutes.

For the sauce, melt the butter in a saucepan, add the flour and cook for 1 minute. Remove from the heat and gradually stir in the stock. Return to the heat and bring to the boil, stirring. Beat together the egg and lemon juice, remove sauce from the heat again, and stir in the egg mixture. Serve with the vine leaves.
Serves 6

Stuffed Aubergines (Eggplant)

METRIC/IMPERIAL	AMERICAN
4 medium aubergines	4 medium eggplant
salt – see method	salt – see method
2 tablespoons olive oil	2 tablespoons olive oil
350 g/12 oz minced beef or lamb	$\frac{3}{4}$ lb ground beef or lamb
1 × 298 g/10$\frac{1}{2}$ oz can condensed French onion soup	1 × 10$\frac{1}{2}$ oz can condensed French onion soup
4 tomatoes, skinned and chopped	4 tomatoes, skinned and chopped
pinch of garlic salt	pinch of garlic salt
3 tablespoons oatmeal	3 tablespoons oatmeal
1 tablespoon Worcestershire sauce	1 tablespoon Worcestershire sauce
salt	salt
freshly ground black pepper	freshly ground black pepper
100 g/4 oz cheese, grated	1 cup shredded cheese

Cut the aubergines (eggplant) in half lengthwise and score the cut sides deeply. Sprinkle with salt and leave for 30 to 45 minutes. Rinse and pat dry, then scoop out centre flesh. Chop the flesh roughly.

Heat the oil in a saucepan and sauté the cut side of the aubergines (eggplant) for 1 to 2 minutes, then remove. Add the meat to the pan and cook, stirring, until browned. Add the aubergine (eggplant) flesh and cook for 3 to 4 minutes. Stir in half the soup and all the remaining ingredients except the cheese. Stir well and simmer for 10 to 15 minutes.

Place the aubergine (eggplant) halves in a shallow ovenproof dish and divide the meat mixture between them. Pour round the remainder of the soup. Bake in a moderately hot oven (190°C/375°F, Gas Mark 5) for 20 to 25 minutes. Sprinkle with the cheese and bake for 10 minutes more.
Serves 4

Baked Courgettes with Lamb

METRIC/IMPERIAL	AMERICAN
450 g/1 lb minced lamb	1 lb ground lamb
1 teaspoon dried mint	1 teaspoon dried mint
salt	salt
freshly ground black pepper	freshly ground black pepper
chicken stock to moisten	chicken stock to moisten
750 g/1$\frac{1}{2}$ lb courgettes, sliced	1$\frac{1}{2}$ lb zucchini, sliced
2 onions, sliced	2 onions, sliced
2 tablespoons oil	2 tablespoons oil
3 tomatoes, sliced	3 tomatoes, sliced
Topping:	**Topping:**
50 g/2 oz fresh brown breadcrumbs	1 cup soft brown bread crumbs
50 g/2 oz Cheddar cheese, grated	$\frac{1}{2}$ cup shredded Cheddar cheese
$\frac{1}{2}$ teaspoon paprika	$\frac{1}{2}$ teaspoon mild paprika

In a bowl, mix the meat with the mint, salt and pepper and moisten with a little stock. Place in the bottom of a large ovenproof dish. In a large saucepan, sauté the courgettes (zucchini) and onions in the oil until just softened, and place on top of the meat. Level the surface and cover with the tomatoes. Mix together the topping ingredients and sprinkle over the tomatoes. Bake in a preheated moderately hot oven (190°C/375°F, Gas Mark 5) for 40 to 45 minutes, until topping is crisp and golden.
Serves 4 to 6

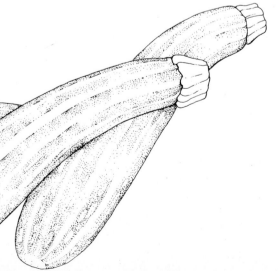

Stuffed Marrow with Tomato Sauce

METRIC/IMPERIAL
25 g/1 oz butter or
  margarine
1 onion, chopped
1 rasher streaky
  bacon, chopped
350 g/12 oz minced
  beef
½ teaspoon dried
  mixed herbs
1 × 298 g/10½ oz can
  condensed tomato
  soup
50 g/2 oz fresh
  breadcrumbs
salt
freshly ground black
  pepper
1 medium marrow
  (about 1 kg/2¼ lb)
150 ml/¼ pint water
2 tablespoons
  chopped parsley

AMERICAN
2 tablespoons butter
  or margarine
1 onion, chopped
1 fat bacon slice,
  chopped
¾ lb ground beef
½ teaspoon dried
  mixed herbs
1 × 10½ oz can
  condensed tomato
  soup
1 cup soft bread
  crumbs
salt
freshly ground black
  pepper
1 medium squash,
  about 2¼ lb
⅔ cup water
2 tablespoons
  chopped parsley

In a saucepan, melt the butter or margarine and sauté the onion and bacon until the onion is transparent. Add the meat and cook, stirring, until browned. Add the herbs and half the soup. Bring to the boil, stirring, reduce the heat and simmer gently for 30 to 35 minutes. Add the breadcrumbs and salt and pepper to taste.

Peel the marrow (squash), cut in half lengthwise and remove the seeds, leaving a shell about 2.5 cm/1 inch thick. Fill each half with meat mixture and sandwich together.

Grease a large piece of foil and wrap round the marrow (squash), sealing well. Place in a roasting tin (pan) and bake in a preheated moderate oven (180°C/350°F, Gas Mark 4) for 1 hour. Fold back the foil and cook for a further 15 to 20 minutes to brown.

In a small saucepan, heat the water with the remainder of the soup, add the parsley and serve with the stuffed marrow (squash).
Serves 6

Southern French Gratin

METRIC/IMPERIAL
225 g/8 oz minced
  beef
225 g/8 oz minced
  pork
1 onion, chopped
1 clove garlic, crushed
225 g/8 oz courgettes,
  sliced
1 aubergine, diced
1 × 397 g/14 oz can
  tomatoes
½ teaspoon dried
  thyme
½ teaspoon dried
  rosemary
salt
freshly ground black
  pepper
200 g/7 oz long-grain
  rice
600 ml/1 pint beef
  stock
4 tablespoons grated
  cheese

AMERICAN
½ lb ground beef
½ lb ground pork
1 onion, chopped
1 clove garlic, crushed
½ lb zucchini, sliced
1 eggplant, diced
1 × 14 oz can
  tomatoes
½ teaspoon dried
  thyme
½ teaspoon dried
  rosemary
salt
freshly ground black
  pepper
1 cup long-grain rice
2½ cups beef stock
4 tablespoons
  shredded cheese

In a large frying pan (skillet), gently fry the beef and pork without additional fat until browned. Add the onion, garlic, courgettes (zucchini) and aubergine (eggplant). Add the tomatoes together with the spices and salt and pepper to taste. Mix well, cover and simmer for 35 minutes. Put rice and stock into a saucepan. Bring to the boil and stir once. Lower heat to simmer, cover and cook for 15 minutes, or until rice is tender and liquid absorbed. Mix the rice with the vegetable and meat mixture and place in a shallow ovenproof dish, sprinkle with the cheese and place under a preheated grill (broiler) for 10 minutes.
Serves 6

Southern French Gratin
(Photograph: US Rice Council)

Stuffed Cabbage Leaves

METRIC/IMPERIAL
1 tablespoon oil
1 onion, chopped
350 g/12 oz minced
  beef
50 g/2 oz cooked rice
2 tablespoons
  chopped parsley
pinch of ground
  allspice
2 teaspoons lemon
  juice
salt
freshly ground black
  pepper
4 tablespoons soured
  cream
8–10 large cabbage
  leaves
beef stock
1 × 300 g/10½ oz can
  tomato and
  mushroom
  spaghetti sauce

AMERICAN
1 tablespoon oil
1 onion, chopped
¾ lb ground beef
½ cup cooked rice
2 tablespoons
  chopped parsley
pinch of ground
  allspice
2 teaspoons lemon
  juice
salt
freshly ground black
  pepper
4 tablespoons sour
  cream
8–10 large cabbage
  leaves
beef stock
1 × 10½ oz can tomato
  and mushroom
  spaghetti sauce

Heat the oil in a saucepan and sauté the onion until soft. Add the meat and brown well. Place in a bowl and add the rice, parsley, spice and lemon juice. Season with salt and pepper to taste, add the sour cream and mix well. Blanch the cabbage leaves for 2 to 3 minutes in boiling salted water. Drain and remove any hard stalks. Divide the filling mixture between the leaves, roll up and place join side down in a shallow ovenproof dish.

Pour in sufficient stock to come halfway up the leaves, cover and bake in a preheated moderate oven (180°C/350°F, Gas Mark 4) for about 45 minutes. Lift out the leaves with a slotted spoon and place on a warm serving dish. Heat the spaghetti sauce and pour over.
Serves 4 to 5

Continental Stuffed Cabbage

METRIC/IMPERIAL
1 fairly firm green
  cabbage
225 g/8 oz minced
  lamb or beef
200 g/7 oz cooked rice
3 tablespoons tomato
  purée
2 teaspoons German
  mustard
salt
freshly ground black
  pepper
2 cloves garlic,
  crushed
300 ml/½ pint chicken
  stock

AMERICAN
1 fairly firm green
  cabbage
½ lb ground lamb or
  beef
1¾ cups cooked rice
3 tablespoons tomato
  paste
2 teaspoons mild
  mustard
salt
freshly ground black
  pepper
2 cloves garlic,
  crushed
1¼ cups chicken stock

Trim the outside leaves from the cabbage. Cut a 2.5 cm/1 inch slice off the top and cut out the middle, leaving a shell about 2.5 cm/1 inch thick. Blanch the cabbage in boiling salted water for 2 to 3 minutes and drain. Shred the centre of the cabbage and blanch. Drain.

Fry the meat over high heat until browned. Add the rice, 1 tablespoon tomato purée (paste), mustard, salt and pepper, garlic and shredded cabbage and mix well.

Stuff the mixture into the cabbage shell and place it in a large saucepan. Mix the stock with the remaining tomato purée (paste) and pour round the cabbage. Cover tightly and simmer gently for 20 to 25 minutes, until cabbage is just cooked.
Serves 4

Veal and Spinach Bake

METRIC/IMPERIAL	AMERICAN
2 × 225 g/8 oz packets frozen spinach, thawed	2 × ½ lb packets frozen spinach, thawed
salt	salt
freshly ground black pepper	freshly ground black pepper
¼ teaspoon ground nutmeg	¼ teaspoon ground nutmeg
450 g/1 lb minced veal	1 lb ground veal
225 g/8 oz curd or cottage cheese	1 cup curd or cottage cheese
Topping:	**Topping:**
300 ml/½ pint plain yogurt	1¼ cups plain yogurt
2 eggs, beaten	2 eggs, beaten
grated nutmeg	grated nutmeg

Place the spinach in a strainer and press to remove excess water. Season with salt, pepper and nutmeg.

Season the meat with salt and pepper, then place alternate layers of spinach, cheese and veal in a greased ovenproof dish.

Beat together the yogurt and eggs and pour over the veal. Sprinkle with nutmeg and bake in a preheated moderate oven (180°C/350°F, Gas Mark 4) for 45 to 50 minutes, until golden.
Serves 4 to 6

Spicy Stuffed Peppers

METRIC/IMPERIAL	AMERICAN
4 large peppers	4 large peppers
450 g/1 lb minced pork	1 lb ground pork
grated rind and juice of 1 lemon	grated rind and juice of 1 lemon
90 g/3½ oz long-grain rice	½ cup long-grain rice
2 teaspoons Dijon mustard	2 teaspoons Dijon-style mustard
salt	salt
freshly ground black pepper	freshly ground black pepper
1 teaspoon sugar	1 teaspoon sugar
2 tablespoons oil	2 tablespoons oil
2 tablespoons tomato purée	2 tablespoons tomato paste
250 ml/8 fl oz chicken stock	1 cup chicken stock

Cut the tops off the peppers and remove the seeds. Blanch the peppers and the tops in boiling salted water for 5 minutes, then drain upside down on kitchen paper. Mix the meat, lemon juice and rind, rice, mustard, salt and pepper and sugar and stir well. Divide between the peppers. Heat the oil in a saucepan just large enough to hold the peppers upright. Mix the tomato purée (paste) with the stock and spoon some of this mixture over each pepper. Cover with the reserved tops. Reduce heat to low, cover the pan and simmer for 45 minutes until the peppers are tender and the rice cooked.
Serves 4

Baked Marrow Surprise

METRIC/IMPERIAL	AMERICAN
1 marrow (about 1 kg/ 2¼ lb)	1 squash, about 2¼ lb
350 g/12 oz minced beef	¾ lb ground beef
1 onion, chopped	1 onion, chopped
1 tablespoon tomato purée	1 tablespoon tomato paste
1 × 447 g/15¾ oz can baked beans	1 × 16 oz can baked beans
2 teaspoons dried mixed herbs	2 teaspoons dried mixed herbs
4 tablespoons rolled oats	4 tablespoons rolled oats
salt	salt
freshly ground black pepper	freshly ground black pepper
1 orange, sliced	1 orange, sliced

Cut a rectangular lid out of one side of the marrow (squash) and scoop out all the seeds. Mix the meat with the onion, tomato purée (paste), baked beans, herbs and oats. Add salt and pepper to taste and pack into the marrow (squash) shell. Cut the lid into four pieces and replace on the marrow (squash) with the orange slices arranged in between.

Wrap the marrow (squash) in greased foil, place in a roasting tin (pan) and bake in a preheated moderately hot oven (200°C/400°F, Gas Mark 6) for about 1¼ hours until cooked.
Serves 4 to 6

Family Dishes

Beef Rice Peasant Style

METRIC/IMPERIAL	AMERICAN
1 tablespoon oil	1 tablespoon oil
1 large onion, chopped	1 large onion, chopped
1 clove garlic, crushed	1 clove garlic, crushed
4 medium carrots, cut into chunks	4 medium carrots, cut into chunks
450 g/1 lb minced beef	1 lb ground beef
1 × 225 g/8 oz can tomatoes	1 × 8 oz can tomatoes
1 tablespoon tomato purée	1 tablespoon tomato paste
1 bay leaf	1 bay leaf
salt	salt
freshly ground black pepper	freshly ground black pepper
200 g/7 oz long-grain rice	1 cup long-grain rice
600 ml/1 pint water	2½ cups water
1 teaspoon salt	1 teaspoon salt

Heat the oil in a saucepan and sauté the onion and the garlic until soft. Add the carrots and the meat and cook, stirring, until the meat is well browned. Add the tomatoes, tomato purée (paste), bay leaf and salt and pepper to taste. Simmer for 25 to 30 minutes, until thickened.

Meanwhile put the rice, water and salt into a saucepan, bring to the boil and stir. Cover and simmer for 15 minutes, until the rice is tender and the water absorbed. Place on a warmed serving dish. Remove the bay leaf from the meat mixture and pour over the rice.
Serves 4

Beef Rice Peasant Style
(Photograph US Rice Council)

Beef and Bean Cobbler

METRIC/IMPERIAL	AMERICAN
1 tablespoon oil	1 tablespoon oil
1 onion, chopped	1 onion, chopped
350 g/12 oz minced beef	¾ lb ground beef
1 × 225 g/8 oz can tomatoes	1 × 8 oz can tomatoes
1 × 447 g/15¾ oz can baked beans	1 × 16 oz can baked beans
1 × 400 g/14 oz can black-eye beans	1 × 14 oz can black-eye beans
175 g/6 oz smoked Dutch sausage, diced	6 oz smoked pork sausage, diced
Topping:	**Topping:**
225 g/8 oz self-raising flour	2 cups self-rising flour
pinch of salt	pinch of salt
50 g/2 oz margarine	¼ cup margarine
150 ml/¼ pint milk	⅔ cup milk
beaten egg to glaze	beaten egg to glaze

Heat the oil in a large saucepan and sauté the onion until soft. Add the meat and cook until well browned. Add all the remaining ingredients (except for topping), bring to the boil, reduce heat and simmer gently for 15 minutes, until thickened. Transfer to an ovenproof dish. For the topping, sift together the flour and salt and rub (cut) in the margarine until the mixture resembles fine breadcrumbs. Add enough milk to form a slightly soft dough, roll out to 1 cm/½ inch thick and cut out rounds with a 5 cm/2 inch cutter. Arrange these round the edge of the dish, overlapping if necessary, and brush with egg. Bake in a preheated moderately hot oven (200°C/400°F, Gas Mark 6) for 25 to 30 minutes until the topping is golden.
Serves 4 to 6

Beef Bake with Beer

METRIC/IMPERIAL
15 g/½ oz margarine
450 g/1 lb minced beef
1 × 225 g/8 oz packet
  frozen mixed
  vegetables
200 ml/⅓ pint beef
  stock
300 ml/½ pint brown
  ale
100 g/4 oz
  mushrooms,
  chopped
salt
freshly ground black
  pepper
Topping:
2 tomatoes, skinned
  and sliced
salt
freshly ground black
  pepper
450 g/1 lb potatoes,
  sliced thinly
50 g/2 oz margarine
300 ml/½ pint plain
  yogurt
¼ teaspoon ground
  nutmeg
50 g/2 oz grated
  cheese

AMERICAN
1 tablespoon
  margarine
1 lb ground beef
1 × ½ lb packet frozen
  mixed vegetables
⅞ cup beef stock
1¼ cups dark beer
1 cup chopped
  mushrooms
salt
freshly ground black
  pepper
Topping:
2 tomatoes, peeled
  and sliced
salt
freshly ground black
  pepper
1 lb potatoes, sliced
  thinly
¼ cup margarine
1¼ cups plain yogurt
¼ teaspoon ground
  nutmeg
½ cup shredded cheese

Melt the margarine in a saucepan and sauté the meat for 5 to 10 minutes until browned. Add the vegetables, stock, brown ale and mushrooms. Add salt and pepper to taste and simmer for 30 minutes. Turn into an ovenproof dish and arrange the tomatoes on top. Sprinkle with salt and pepper. Fry the potatoes in the margarine until softened and arrange over the tomatoes. Combine the yogurt and nutmeg and pour over the potatoes. Sprinkle with the cheese and bake in a preheated moderately hot oven (200°C/400°F, Gas Mark 6) for 25 to 30 minutes until the top is browned.
Serves 4

Beef and Tomato Layer Pie

METRIC/IMPERIAL
450 g/1 lb minced beef
1 onion, chopped
50 g/2 oz bran cereal
1 tablespoon
  Worcestershire
  sauce
salt
freshly ground black
  pepper
350 g/12 oz plain flour
salt
175 g/6 oz margarine
cold water to mix
2 eggs, hard-boiled
  and sliced
2 tomatoes, sliced
2 tablespoons
  chopped parsley
salt
freshly ground black
  pepper
beaten egg or milk to
  glaze

AMERICAN
1 lb ground beef
1 onion, chopped
½ cup bran cereal
1 tablespoon
  Worcestershire
  sauce
salt
freshly ground black
  pepper
3 cups all-purpose
  flour
salt
¾ cup margarine
cold water to mix
2 eggs, hard-cooked
  and sliced
2 tomatoes, sliced
2 tablespoons
  chopped parsley
salt
freshly ground black
  pepper
beaten egg or milk to
  glaze

Cook the meat and onion in a saucepan over a low heat without any additional fat until the meat is brown and the onion soft. Stir in the cereal, Worcestershire sauce and salt and pepper. Mix well and allow to cool.

Sift the flour and salt into a basin and rub (cut) in the margarine until the mixture resembles fine breadcrumbs. Stir in enough cold water to make a stiff dough.

Roll out just over half the pastry (dough) to line a 24 cm/9½ inch loose-based flan tin (pie pan). Place half the meat mixture over the pastry (dough), cover with eggs and tomatoes then top with parsley and salt and pepper. Place the remaining meat mixture on top and roll out remaining pastry (dough) to cover the pie, sealing the edges well. Decorate with pastry (dough) trimmings, brush with egg or milk to glaze and bake in a preheated moderately hot oven (190°C/375°F, Gas Mark 5) for 50 minutes.
Serves 6

Beef Curry

METRIC/IMPERIAL	AMERICAN
450 g/1 lb minced beef	1 lb ground beef
1 onion, chopped	1 onion, chopped
1 cooking apple, peeled, cored and chopped	1 large apple, peeled, cored and chopped
3 tablespoons curry powder	3 tablespoons curry powder
2 teaspoons curry paste	2 teaspoons curry paste
25 g/1 oz plain flour	$\frac{1}{4}$ cup all-purpose flour
900 ml/1½ pints beef stock	3¾ cups beef stock
2 tablespoons tomato purée	2 tablespoons tomato paste
juice of half a lemon	juice of half a lemon
1 tablespoon mango chutney	1 tablespoon mango chutney

Fry the meat in a saucepan without additional fat until it is well browned. Add the onion and apple and cook gently for 5 minutes, being careful not to let the apple and onion brown. Stir in the curry powder and paste and cook for a further 5 minutes. Stir in the flour and gradually add the stock. Bring to the boil, stirring, until the mixture thickens. Add the tomato purée (paste), lemon juice and mango chutney. Reduce heat, cover and simmer for 45 minutes.
Serves 4

Okra Lamb Casserole

METRIC/IMPERIAL	AMERICAN
1 tablespoon oil	1 tablespoon oil
450 g/1 lb minced raw lamb	1 lb ground lamb
1 × 397 g/14 oz can tomatoes	1 × 14 oz can tomatoes
salt	salt
freshly ground black pepper	freshly ground black pepper
1 × 411 g/14½ oz can okra, rinsed and drained	1 × 14½ oz can okra, rinsed and drained
juice of 2 lemons	juice of 2 lemons

Heat the oil in a saucepan and sauté the meat until browned. Add the remaining ingredients, stir well, cover and simmer for 45 minutes until the meat is tender.
Serves 4

Minced Collops

METRIC/IMPERIAL	AMERICAN
25 g/1 oz dripping	2 tablespoons drippings
1 large onion, chopped	1 large onion, chopped
450 g/1 lb minced beef	1 lb ground beef
2 tablespoons medium oatmeal	2 tablespoons medium oatmeal
300 ml/½ pint beef stock	1¼ cups beef stock
1 tablespoon tomato ketchup	1 tablespoon tomato ketchup
1 tablespoon Yorkshire relish	1 tablespoon sweet pickle relish
salt	salt
freshly ground black pepper	freshly ground black pepper

Melt the dripping in a saucepan and sauté the onion until soft. Add the meat and cook, stirring, until well browned. Add the remaining ingredients. Stir well. Bring to the boil, reduce heat, cover and simmer for about 30 minutes.
Serves 4

Witches' Broth

METRIC/IMPERIAL	AMERICAN
50 g/2 oz margarine	$\frac{1}{4}$ cup margarine
1 onion, chopped	1 onion, chopped
1 red or green pepper, cored, seeded and chopped	1 red or green pepper, cored, seeded and chopped
225 g/8 oz minced beef	8 oz ground beef
1 × 397 g/14 oz can tomatoes	1 × 14 oz can tomatoes
600 ml/1 pint beef stock	2½ cups beef stock
½ teaspoon chilli powder	½ teaspoon chili powder
salt	salt
1 × 439 g/15½ oz can red kidney beans	1 × 16 oz can red kidney beans

Melt the margarine in a large saucepan and sauté the onion and pepper until soft. Add the meat and continue frying until well browned. Stir in the tomatoes, stock, chilli powder and salt. Bring to the boil, reduce heat and simmer for about 30 minutes. Add the beans and reheat. Serve with crusty bread.
Serves 4

Bobotie

METRIC/IMPERIAL	AMERICAN
1 slice white bread	1 slice white bread
450 ml/¾ pint milk	2 cups milk
2 tablespoons corn oil	2 tablespoons corn oil
1 onion, chopped	1 onion, chopped
450 g/1 lb minced beef	1 lb ground beef
1 tablespoon curry powder	1 tablespoon curry powder
1 teaspoon turmeric	1 teaspoon turmeric
2 beef stock cubes, crumbled	4 beef bouillon cubes, crumbled
1 tablespoon vinegar	1 tablespoon vinegar
3 bay leaves	3 bay leaves
1 egg	1 egg
350 g/12 oz long-grain rice	1½ cups long-grain rice
900 ml/1½ pints water	3¾ cups water
½ teaspoon salt	½ teaspoon salt
pinch of saffron	pinch of saffron
100 g/4 oz seedless raisins	¾ cup seedless raisins

Soak the bread in 150 ml/¼ pint (⅔ cup) milk. Mix the remaining milk with water to make 600 ml/1 pint (2½ cups). Heat the oil in a saucepan then sauté the onion lightly. Add the meat and brown well. Add the curry powder, turmeric, stock (bouillon) cubes, and vinegar. Cook for a few minutes. Mash the bread with the milk and add to the meat with the bay leaves. Place the mixture in a casserole.

Beat the egg with the milk and water mixture and pour over the meat. Bake in the centre of a moderate oven (180°C/350°F, Gas Mark 4) for about 30 minutes, until the meat is firm and the custard topping has set. Meanwhile, put the rice, water, salt and saffron into a saucepan, bring to the boil and stir once. Reduce heat, cover and simmer for 15 minutes, until the rice is tender and the liquid absorbed. Stir in the raisins just before the rice is cooked. Serve with the bobotie.
Serves 4 to 6

Shepherd's Pie

METRIC/IMPERIAL	AMERICAN
25 g/1 oz dripping	2 tablespoons drippings
1 small onion, chopped	1 small onion, chopped
50 g/2 oz mushrooms, chopped	½ cup chopped mushrooms
450 g/1 lb minced lamb or beef	1 lb ground lamb or beef
15 g/½ oz plain flour	2 tablespoons all-purpose flour
300 ml/½ pint beef stock	1¼ cups beef stock
1 teaspoon Worcestershire sauce	1 teaspoon Worcestershire sauce
1 egg, beaten	1 egg, beaten
450 g/1 lb potatoes, mashed	2 cups mashed potato

Melt the dripping in a saucepan and sauté the onion and mushrooms until soft and golden. Add the meat and continue cooking for 5 minutes, stirring well. Sprinkle in the flour and cook for 1 minute. Gradually add the stock. Continue stirring over a low heat for 5 minutes. Season with the Worcestershire sauce and place in an ovenproof dish.

Add half the egg to the potatoes and mix well. Place on the meat, mark in lines with a fork and brush with remaining egg. Bake in a preheated moderately hot oven (200°C/400°F, Gas Mark 6) for 40 minutes.
Serves 4

Shepherd's Pie
(Photograph: Bovril Cubes)

Pork and Parsnip Layer Pie

METRIC/IMPERIAL	AMERICAN
450 g/1 lb minced pork	1 lb ground pork
1 onion, finely chopped	1 onion, finely chopped
1 carrot, grated	1 carrot, grated
25 g/1 oz bran cereal	$\frac{1}{4}$ cup bran cereal
1 tablespoon Worcestershire sauce	1 tablespoon Worcestershire sauce
few drops Tabasco sauce	few drops hot pepper sauce
salt	salt
freshly ground black pepper	freshly ground black pepper
350 g/12 oz wholewheat flour	3 cups wholewheat flour
175 g/6 oz margarine	$\frac{3}{4}$ cup margarine
cold water to mix	cold water to mix
1 medium parsnip, thinly sliced	1 medium parsnip, thinly sliced
1 × 225 g/8 oz can tomatoes, drained	1 × 8 oz can tomatoes, drained

Cook the meat, onion and carrot in a saucepan over a low heat without any additional fat until the meat is brown and the vegetables are tender, stirring frequently. Stir in the cereal, Worcestershire sauce, Tabasco (hot pepper sauce) and salt and pepper. Mix well and allow to cool.

Sift the flour and a pinch of salt into a bowl. Rub (cut) in the margarine until the mixture resembles fine breadcrumbs. Stir in sufficient water to form a stiff dough. Roll out just over half the pastry and use to line a 24 cm/9$\frac{1}{2}$ inch loose-based flan tin (pie pan). Place half the meat mixture on the pastry (dough), cover with the sliced parsnip and tomatoes, and top with the remaining meat mixture.

Roll out the rest of the pastry (dough) and use to cover the pie, sealing the edges well. Decorate with pastry (dough) trimmings and brush with egg or milk to glaze. Bake in a preheated moderately hot oven (190°C/375°F, Gas Mark 5) for 50 minutes.
Serves 4

Mortine's Beef Rice

METRIC/IMPERIAL	AMERICAN
1 tablespoon oil	1 tablespoon oil
1 teaspoon chilli powder	1 teaspoon chili powder
1 teaspoon salt	1 teaspoon salt
$\frac{1}{2}$ teaspoon freshly ground black pepper	$\frac{1}{2}$ teaspoon freshly ground black pepper
$\frac{1}{2}$ teaspoon garlic salt	$\frac{1}{2}$ teaspoon garlic salt
600 ml/1 pint chicken stock	2$\frac{1}{2}$ cups chicken stock
200 g/7 oz long-grain rice	1 cup long-grain rice
pinch of dried thyme	pinch of dried thyme
1 tablespoon oil	1 tablespoon oil
1 large onion, chopped	1 large onion, chopped
275 g/10 oz minced beef	1$\frac{1}{4}$ cups firmly packed ground beef
1 leek, sliced	1 leek, sliced
100 g/4 oz frozen peas, cooked	$\frac{3}{4}$ cup frozen peas, cooked
1 × 198 g/7 oz can sweetcorn	1 × 7 oz can whole kernel corn
1 red pepper, cored, seeded and chopped	1 red pepper, cored, seeded and chopped
1 tablespoon chopped parsley to garnish	1 tablespoon chopped parsley to garnish

Heat the oil in a saucepan and gently sauté the chilli powder, salt, pepper and garlic salt for 2 to 3 minutes. Add the stock, rice and thyme and bring to the boil. Reduce heat, stir, cover and simmer for 15 minutes, or until the rice is tender and the liquid absorbed. Meanwhile, heat the oil in a frying pan (skillet) and sauté the onion and the meat until lightly browned. Add the leek and cook for a further 5 to 10 minutes. Stir in the peas, corn and pepper and heat through.

Mix the meat mixture with the rice, place on a warmed serving dish and sprinkle with chopped parsley.
Serves 4 to 6

Quick Beef Pizzas

METRIC/IMPERIAL	AMERICAN
225 g/8 oz self-raising flour	2 cups self-rising flour
1 teaspoon salt	1 teaspoon salt
65 g/2½ oz butter	⅓ cup butter
150 ml/¼ pint milk	⅔ cup milk
1 large onion, sliced	1 large onion, sliced
1 clove garlic, crushed	1 clove garlic, crushed
1 × 418 g/14¾ oz can minced beef	1 × 15 oz can ground beef
½ teaspoon mixed herbs	½ teaspoon mixed herbs
50 g/2 oz grated Cheddar cheese	½ cup shredded Cheddar cheese
4 slices tomato	4 slices tomato

Sift flour and salt into a bowl. Rub (cut) in 50 g/ 2 oz (¼ cup) of the butter until the mixture resembles fine breadcrumbs. Add the milk and mix to a soft dough. Divide into four and roll each piece to an 18 cm/7 inch circle. Place on a greased baking sheet.

Melt the remaining butter in a saucepan and sauté the onion and garlic until soft. Add the meat and herbs and heat through. Spoon the mixture onto the dough circles and sprinkle with the cheese. Top each with a tomato slice and bake in a preheated moderately hot oven (200°C/400°F, Gas Mark 6) for 15 to 20 minutes.
Serves 4

Southern Hash

METRIC/IMPERIAL	AMERICAN
450 g/1 lb minced pork	1 lb ground pork
1 large onion, chopped	1 large onion, chopped
1 green pepper, cored, seeded and chopped	1 green pepper, cored, seeded and chopped
1 tablespoon oil	1 tablespoon oil
400 g/14 oz long-grain rice	2 cups long-grain rice
1 × 397 g/14 oz can tomatoes	1 × 14 oz can tomatoes
beef stock	beef stock
1 tablespoon chilli powder	1 tablespoon chili powder
salt	salt
freshly ground black pepper	freshly ground black pepper
450 g/1 lb frozen green beans	1 lb frozen green beans

In a flameproof casserole, sauté the meat, onion and green pepper in the oil until the meat is lightly browned. Stir in the rice and cook for a further 2 minutes.

Drain the tomatoes and make the juice up to 900 ml/1½ pints (3¾ cups) with stock. Add to the pan with the tomatoes, chilli powder, salt and pepper and beans. Heat until boiling, stir well, cover and place in a preheated moderate oven (180°C/350°F, Gas Mark 4). Cook until rice is tender, about 40 minutes.
Serves 4 to 6

Crispy-Topped Wine Bake

METRIC/IMPERIAL	AMERICAN
1 tablespoon olive oil	1 tablespoon olive oil
225 g/8 oz button onions, peeled	½ lb pearl onions, peeled
100 g/4 oz fat bacon, diced	¼ lb fat bacon, diced
450 g/1 lb lean minced beef	1 lb lean ground beef
300 ml/½ pint red wine	1¼ cups red wine
300 ml/½ pint beef stock	1¼ cups beef stock
1 bouquet garni	1 bouquet garni
salt	salt
freshly ground black pepper	freshly ground black pepper
Topping:	**Topping:**
50 g/2 oz butter	¼ cup butter
2 cloves garlic, crushed	2 cloves garlic, crushed
8 slices French bread	8 slices French bread

Heat the oil in a flameproof casserole and sauté the onions slowly until well browned. Remove onions with a slotted spoon and set aside.

Add the bacon to the remaining oil in the pan and fry briskly for 5 to 6 minutes. Add the meat and continue cooking, stirring, until well browned.

Stir in the wine and stock. Add the reserved onions, bouquet garni and salt and pepper. Cover and cook in a preheated moderate oven (180°C/350°F, Gas Mark 4) for 1½ hours.

For the topping, soften the butter and work in the garlic. Spread on the slices of bread. Remove the casserole from the oven and raise oven temperature to moderately hot (200°C/ 400°F, Gas Mark 6). Arrange the French bread slices on top of the meat and return to the oven, uncovered, for 15 minutes.
Serves 4

Meat Loaves

Picnic Pork Paté

METRIC/IMPERIAL
225 g/8 oz streaky bacon, rind removed
450 g/1 lb pork liver
350 g/12 oz lean pork
225 g/8 oz sausagemeat
2 egg yolks
150 ml/¼ pint double cream
3 tablespoons mild mustard
1 small onion, chopped
1 teaspoon dried sage
1 teaspoon marjoram
salt
freshly ground black pepper

AMERICAN
½ lb streaky bacon, rind removed
1 lb pork liver
¾ lb lean pork
½ lb sausagemeat
2 egg yolks
⅔ cup heavy cream
3 tablespoons mild mustard
1 small onion, chopped
1 teaspoon dried sage
1 teaspoon marjoram
salt
freshly ground black pepper

Stretch the rashers (slices) of bacon with the back of a knife and use to line a 1 kg/2 lb loaf tin (9 × 5 inch loaf pan). Mince (grind) the liver and pork together. Mix with the remaining ingredients. Pour into the tin (pan) and smooth the top. Cover with any remaining bacon.

Cover with a double thickness of foil and stand in a roasting tin (pan) of hot water. Bake in a preheated moderate oven (180°C/350°F, Gas Mark 4) for 1½ hours. Remove from oven, remove foil, and pour off excess fat. Place a weight on top and allow to cool. Turn out of tin (pan) and chill before serving.
Serves 8 to 10

Mushroom Meat Loaf

METRIC/IMPERIAL
350 g/12 oz minced beef
100 g/4 oz minced pork
100 g/4 oz mushrooms, finely chopped
2 sticks celery, finely chopped
100 g/4 oz fresh breadcrumbs
1 egg, beaten
1 tablespoon dried chopped onion
1 teaspoon dry mustard
a little beef stock (optional)
freshly ground black pepper

AMERICAN
¾ lb ground beef
¼ lb ground pork
1 cup finely chopped mushrooms
2 stalks celery, finely chopped
2 cups soft bread crumbs
1 egg, beaten
1 tablespoon dried chopped onion
1 teaspoon dry mustard
a little beef stock (optional)
freshly ground black pepper

Place all ingredients in a large bowl and mix well together, adding a little beef stock if the mixture seems dry.

Place in a well greased 1 kg/2 lb loaf tin (9 × 5 inch loaf pan) and bake in a preheated moderately hot oven (190°C/375°F, Gas Mark 5) for 1 hour.
Serves 4

Picnic Pork Paté
(Photograph: Colman's Mustard)

Stuffed Meat Loaf with Mushroom and Tomato Sauce

METRIC/IMPERIAL
3 tablespoons sage and onion stuffing mix
5 tablespoons boiling water
1 medium onion, chopped
450 g/1 lb minced beef
25 g/1 oz fresh breadcrumbs
1 egg, beaten
1 tablespoon chop or bottled brown sauce
salt
freshly ground black pepper
Sauce:
1 × 298 g/10½ oz can condensed mushroom soup
2 tablespoons tomato ketchup
1 teaspoon Worcestershire sauce
6 tablespoons water

AMERICAN
3 tablespoons sage and onion stuffing mix
⅓ cup boiling water
1 medium onion, chopped
1 lb ground beef
½ cup soft bread crumbs
1 egg, beaten
1 tablespoon chop or bottled brown sauce
salt
freshly ground black pepper
Sauce:
1 × 10½ oz can condensed mushroom soup
2 tablespoons tomato ketchup
1 teaspoon Worcestershire sauce
6 tablespoons water

In a small bowl, mix the stuffing mix and water, making the stuffing slightly stiffer than usual. Allow to cool. In a bowl, combine the onion, meat, breadcrumbs, egg, chop sauce, and salt and pepper and mix well. Grease a 450 g/1 lb loaf tin (7 × 3 inch loaf pan). Spoon in half the meat mixture and press down well. Put the stuffing on top of the meat and level the surface, then top with the remaining meat mixture. Cover with foil and bake in a moderately hot oven (200°C/400°F, Gas Mark 6) for 30 minutes. Remove the foil and cook for a further 15 to 20 minutes. Meanwhile, mix all the sauce ingredients in a saucepan, and heat gently until boiling. Turn the meat loaf onto a serving plate and serve the sauce separately.
Serves 4

Picnic Loaf with Barbeque Sauce

METRIC/IMPERIAL
450 g/1 lb minced pork
225 g/½ lb minced veal
2 eggs, beaten
4 tablespoons milk
350 g/12 oz cooked long-grain rice (125 g/4 oz uncooked)
1 medium onion, grated
1 tablespoon Yorkshire relish or pickle
salt
freshly ground black pepper
100 g/4 oz Edam cheese, thinly sliced
Sauce:
4 tablespoons tomato ketchup
1 teaspoon mustard
1 teaspoon brown sugar
1 teaspoon lemon juice
1 teaspoon soy sauce

AMERICAN
1 lb ground pork
½ lb ground veal
2 eggs, beaten
¼ cup milk
2 cups cooked long-grain rice (⅔ cup uncooked)
1 medium onion, grated
1 tablespoon sweet pickle relish
salt
freshly ground black pepper
¼ lb Edam cheese, thinly sliced
Sauce:
¼ cup tomato ketchup
1 teaspoon mustard
1 teaspoon brown sugar
1 teaspoon lemon juice
1 teaspoon soy sauce

In a large bowl combine the meats, egg, milk, rice, onion, relish, salt and pepper and mix thoroughly. Grease a 1.75 litre/3 pint (2 quart) loaf tin (pan) and press in half the meat mixture. Arrange sliced cheese over the meat then top with remaining mixture. Cook in a moderate oven (180°C/350°F, Gas Mark 4) for 50 minutes or until the meat is cooked. Allow the loaf to cool in the tin (pan) for 10 minutes before turning out. Heat the sauce ingredients in a saucepan and simmer for 5 minutes. Serve loaf and sauce hot or cold as required.
Serves 6

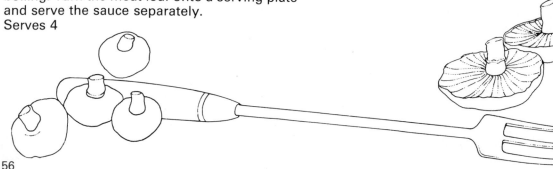

Savoury Meat Roll

METRIC/IMPERIAL	AMERICAN
100 g/4 oz bacon, finely chopped	¼ lb bacon, finely chopped
225 g/8 oz minced beef	½ lb ground beef
75 g/3 oz fresh brown breadcrumbs	1½ cups soft brown bread crumbs
salt	salt
freshly ground black pepper	freshly ground black pepper
1 egg, beaten	1 egg, beaten
1 beef stock cube	2 beef bouillon cubes
2 tablespoons water	2 tablespoons water

Take an empty 450 g/1 lb soup can and remove both ends. In a bowl mix the bacon with the beef, breadcrumbs, salt, pepper and egg. Add the crumbled stock cube and water, and stir well. Stand the can on a large piece of foil and fill with the meat mixture. Bring the foil up over the sides and seal firmly on top.

Steam for two hours and then leave to cool for 15 minutes. Remove the foil and carefully unmould the meat roll onto a serving dish.
Serves 2

Layered Meat Loaf

METRIC/IMPERIAL	AMERICAN
450 g/1 lb minced pork	1 lb ground pork
50 g/2 oz white breadcrumbs	1 cup soft bread crumbs
1 tablespoon tomato purée	1 tablespoon tomato paste
1 egg, beaten	1 egg, beaten
pinch of nutmeg	pinch of nutmeg
pinch of ground cinnamon	pinch of ground cinnamon
salt	salt
freshly ground black pepper	freshly ground black pepper
4 processed cheese slices	4 processed cheese slices

In a bowl, combine the meat, breadcrumbs, tomato purée, egg, spices and seasoning.

Press half the mixture into a well greased 450 g/1 lb loaf tin (7 × 3 inch loaf pan). Cover with the cheese slices, then top with the remaining mixture. Bake in a preheated moderately hot oven (190°C/375°F, Gas Mark 5) for 1 hour. Turn out and serve hot or cold.
Serves 4

Pasta Meat Loaf

METRIC/IMPERIAL	AMERICAN
100 g/4 oz pasta wheels	1 cup pasta wheels
1 tablespoon oil	1 tablespoon oil
1 onion, chopped	1 onion, chopped
450 g/1 lb minced beef	1 lb ground beef
50 g/2 oz cheese, grated	½ cup shredded cheese
2 eggs, beaten	2 eggs, beaten
salt	salt
freshly ground black pepper	freshly ground black pepper
1 teaspoon garlic salt	1 teaspoon garlic salt
2 teaspoons Worcestershire sauce	2 teaspoons Worcestershire sauce
½ teaspoon mixed herbs	½ teaspoon mixed herbs

Cook the pasta in a saucepan with plenty of boiling salted water until tender. Drain.

Heat the oil in a frying pan (skillet) and sauté the onion until soft. Add the meat and continue cooking until well browned.

Remove from the heat and stir in the remaining ingredients. Mix well and place in a well greased 450 g/1 lb loaf tin (7 × 3 inch loaf pan). Bake in a preheated moderate oven (180°C/350°F, Gas Mark 4) for 30 minutes.
Serves 4 to 6

Bran and Bean Meatloaf

METRIC/IMPERIAL	AMERICAN
750 g/1½ lb minced beef	1½ lb ground beef
1 onion, chopped	1 onion, chopped
1 egg, beaten	1 egg, beaten
2 bacon or chicken stock cubes, crumbled	4 bacon or chicken stock cubes, crumbled
1 tablespoon tomato ketchup	1 tablespoon tomato ketchup
75 g/3 oz bran cereal	1 cup bran cereal
1 × 219 g/7¾ oz can baked beans, drained	1 × 8 oz can baked beans, drained

Combine all the ingredients in a large bowl and mix well. Press into a well greased 1 kg/2 lb loaf tin and bake in a preheated moderate oven (180°C/350°F, Gas Mark 4) for 1 to 1¼ hours.
Serves 4 to 6

Burgers

Lamb Burgers

METRIC/IMPERIAL	AMERICAN
25 g/1 oz butter	2 tablespoons butter
1 onion, finely chopped	1 onion, finely chopped
450 g/1 lb minced lamb	1 lb minced lamb
1 stick celery, finely chopped	1 stalk celery, finely chopped
1 tablespoon tomato purée	1 tablespoon tomato paste
1 tablespoon tomato ketchup	1 tablespoon tomato ketchup
1 teaspoon mixed herbs	1 teaspoon mixed herbs
salt	salt
freshly ground black pepper	freshly ground black pepper
50 g/2 oz fresh breadcrumbs	1 cup soft bread crumbs
To serve:	**To serve:**
soft rolls, lettuce and tomatoes	soft rolls, lettuce and tomatoes

Melt the butter in a frying pan (skillet) and sauté the onion. Place in a bowl and add the remaining ingredients. Mix well, divide into four and shape into burgers.

Fry in a lightly greased frying pan (skillet) for about 5 minutes each side until browned and still slightly pink inside. (Cook a little longer if you prefer them well done.) Alternatively, place the burgers under a preheated grill (broiler) for the same time. Serve in the split rolls, garnished with lettuce and tomato.
Serves 4

Hamburgers

METRIC/IMPERIAL	AMERICAN
450 g/1 lb lean minced beef	1 lb lean ground beef
salt	salt
freshly ground black pepper	freshly ground black pepper

Place the meat in a bowl and season generously with salt and pepper. Mix well and shape into 4 burgers. For really firm burgers, press into shape in a 10 cm/4 inch biscuit (cookie) cutter or use a hamburger press.

Fry the hamburgers in a lightly greased frying pan (skillet) for 3 to 5 minutes each side for rare burgers, 7 to 8 minutes each side if you like them well done. Alternatively, place them under a preheated grill (broiler) for the same cooking times.
Variations:
Onion Add half an onion, very finely chopped
Herb Add $\frac{1}{4}$ teaspoon marjoram, a pinch of thyme, $\frac{1}{2}$ teaspoon celery salt and 1 teaspoon dried parsley
Chilli-cheese Add 50 g/2 oz grated cheese ($\frac{1}{2}$ cup shredded cheese), 120 ml/4 fl oz ($\frac{1}{2}$ cup) milk and $\frac{1}{2}$ teaspoon chilli powder
Spicy Add 1 tablespoon whole-grain mustard
Horseradish Add 2 teaspoons prepared horseradish
Serves 4

Lamb Burger
(Photograph: New Zealand Lamb Bureau)

Dutch Burger Rolls with Barbecue Sauce

METRIC/IMPERIAL
Burgers:
350 g/12 oz minced beef
100 g/4 oz white breadcrumbs
1 tablespoon Worcestershire sauce
salt
freshly ground black pepper
beaten egg
50 g/2 oz unsalted butter
Sauce:
1 onion, finely chopped
1 × 397 g/14 oz can tomatoes
1 tablespoon vinegar
1 tablespoon brown sugar
2 teaspoons Worcestershire sauce
1 tablespoon tomato purée
To finish:
4 slices cooked ham
4 slices Edam cheese

AMERICAN
Burgers:
¾ lb ground beef
2 cups soft bread crumbs
1 tablespoon Worcestershire sauce
salt
freshly ground black pepper
beaten egg
¼ cup unsalted butter
Sauce:
1 onion, finely chopped
1 × 14 oz can tomatoes
1 tablespoon vinegar
1 tablespoon brown sugar
2 teaspoons Worcestershire sauce
1 tablespoon tomato paste
To finish:
4 slices cooked ham
4 slices Edam cheese

Mix the meat, breadcrumbs, Worcestershire sauce and salt and pepper together. Bind the mixture with a little beaten egg, divide into four and mould into sausage shapes.

Melt the butter in a frying pan (skillet) and gently fry the burgers until cooked and brown. Remove from the pan with a slotted spoon and keep warm. Make the sauce by frying the onion in the same pan until soft. Add the tomatoes, vinegar, sugar, Worcestershire sauce and tomatoe purée (paste), and cook for about 5 minutes.

Roll a slice of cheese and a slice of ham around each burger, place on a warmed serving dish and pour over the sauce.
Serves 4

Stuffed Burger Rolls

METRIC/IMPERIAL
4 round crusty rolls
225 g/8 oz minced beef
2 rashers lean bacon, finely chopped
1 green pepper, cored and chopped
1 teaspoon tomato ketchup
1 egg, beaten
salt
freshly ground black pepper

AMERICAN
4 round hard rolls
½ lb ground beef
2 lean bacon slices, finely chopped
1 green pepper, cored and chopped
1 teaspoon tomato ketchup
1 egg, beaten
salt
freshly ground black pepper

Cut the tops off the rolls, scoop out the middles and make the scooped-out bread into crumbs. Mix with the remaining ingredients.

Stuff the mixture back into the rolls and replace the lids. Wrap each roll in foil and place on a baking sheet. Cook in a moderately hot oven (190°C/375°F, Gas Mark 5) for 25 to 30 minutes. Serve cold.
Makes 4 rolls

Italian Beef Cakes

METRIC/IMPERIAL
grated rind of 1 lemon
2 teaspoons chopped parsley
2 cloves garlic, crushed
450 g/1 lb minced beef
salt
freshly ground black pepper
¼ teaspoon nutmeg
1 slice white bread
beef stock
1 egg, beaten
plain flour
oil for frying

AMERICAN
grated rind of 1 lemon
2 teaspoons chopped parsley
2 cloves garlic, crushed
1 lb ground beef
salt
freshly ground black pepper
¼ teaspoon nutmeg
1 slice white bread
beef stock
1 egg, beaten
all-purpose flour
oil for frying

In a bowl, mix the lemon rind, parsley and garlic with the meat and season generously with the salt, pepper and nutmeg. Soak the bread in a little stock for a few minutes, squeeze out and add to the meat with the egg.

With floured hands, shape the mixture into 8 to 12 shallow cakes. Heat the oil in a frying pan (skillet) and fry for 3 to 4 minutes each side.
Serves 4

Pickle Burgers

METRIC/IMPERIAL
450 g/1 lb minced beef
1 tablespoon chopped
    parsley
1 tablespoon chopped
    chives
1 onion, finely
    chopped
salt
freshly ground black
    pepper
1 egg, beaten
4 pickled cucumbers
    or gherkins
To coat:
plain flour
beaten egg
crushed Bran flakes
oil for deep frying

AMERICAN
1 lb ground beef
1 tablespoon chopped
    parsley
1 tablespoon chopped
    chives
1 onion, finely
    chopped
salt
freshly ground black
    pepper
1 egg, beaten
4 dill pickles or
    gherkins
To coat:
all-purpose flour
beaten egg
crushed Bran flakes
oil for deep frying

In a bowl mix the meat with the parsley, chives and onion. Season well with salt and pepper. Add the egg and mix well. Divide the mixture into 4, flatten each piece out and place a pickled cucumber on each. Mould the meat carefully round the cucumber to form an oval shape.

Coat the burgers in flour, egg and Bran flakes. Heat the oil in a saucepan and deep fry the burgers for 6 minutes.
Serves 4

Lamb Rissoles

METRIC/IMPERIAL
450 g/1 lb cooked
    lamb, minced
50 g/2 oz Corn flakes,
    crushed
½ teaspoon mixed
    herbs
salt
freshly ground black
    pepper
2 tablespoons tomato
    ketchup
1 teaspoon
    Worcestershire
    sauce
2 eggs, beaten
To coat:
1 egg, beaten
50 g/2 oz Corn flakes,
    crushed
oil for frying

AMERICAN
1 lb cooked lamb,
    ground
2 cups Corn flakes,
    crushed
½ teaspoon mixed
    herbs
salt
freshly ground black
    pepper
2 tablespoons tomato
    ketchup
1 teaspoon
    Worcestershire
    sauce
2 eggs, beaten
To coat:
1 egg, beaten
2 cups Corn flakes,
    crushed
oil for frying

Mix the meat, Corn flakes, herbs and salt and pepper. Bind with the ketchup, Worcestershire sauce and eggs.

Shape into 8 rissoles, coat each in beaten egg and then in crushed Corn flakes. Heat oil in a frying pan (skillet) and shallow fry the rissoles for about 3 minutes each side, until golden.
Serves 4

Quick and Tasty Steaklets

METRIC/IMPERIAL	AMERICAN
25 g/1 oz butter	2 tablespoons butter
4 tablespoons oil	4 tablespoons oil
2 onions, finely chopped	2 onions, finely chopped
225 g/8 oz mushrooms, finely chopped	2 cups finely chopped mushrooms
½ teaspoon dried sage	½ teaspoon dried sage
1 clove garlic, crushed	1 clove garlic, crushed
salt	salt
freshly ground black pepper	freshly ground black pepper
750 g/1½ lb minced beef	1½ lb ground beef

Heat the butter and half the oil in a frying pan (skillet) and gently sauté the onions and mushrooms for 3 to 4 minutes. Mix in the sage and the garlic and cook for a further minute. Allow the mixture to cool and place in a bowl. Mix in the salt, pepper and meat.

Divide the mixture into 8 and shape into rounds. Heat the remaining oil in a frying pan and fry gently for about 5 minutes each side.
Serves 4

Pork and Lentil Burgers

METRIC/IMPERIAL	AMERICAN
100 g/4 oz red lentils	½ cup red lentils
350 g/12 oz minced pork	¾ lb ground pork
50 g/2 oz fresh brown breadcrumbs	1 cup soft brown bread crumbs
1 tablespoon lemon juice	1 tablespoon lemon juice
1 teaspoon chopped marjoram or basil	1 teaspoon chopped marjoram or basil
1 egg, beaten	1 egg, beaten
salt	salt
freshly ground black pepper	freshly ground black pepper
oil for frying	oil for frying

Place the lentils in a saucepan, cover with water, bring to the boil and cook for about 30 minutes until soft. Drain and place in a bowl with the remaining ingredients.

Mix well and shape into 4 burgers. Heat the oil in a shallow pan and fry the burgers gently for 8 minutes each side until well cooked.
Serves 4

Devilled Pork Burgers

METRIC/IMPERIAL	AMERICAN
450 g/1 lb minced pork	1 lb ground pork
50 g/2 oz breadcrumbs	1 cup soft bread crumbs
1 onion, finely chopped	1 onion, finely chopped
1 egg, beaten	1 egg, beaten
salt	salt
freshly ground black pepper	freshly ground black pepper
To coat:	**To coat:**
15 g/½ oz flour	1 tablespoon flour
1 teaspoon dry mustard	1 teaspoon dry mustard
1 teaspoon curry powder	1 teaspoon curry powder
1 egg, beaten	1 egg, beaten
coating crumbs	coating crumbs
oil for frying	oil for frying

In a large bowl combine the meat, breadcrumbs, onion and egg, and season generously with salt and pepper. Shape into 8 burgers. Mix the flour, mustard and curry powder on a plate. Coat the burgers with this mixture then with the egg and crumbs. In a frying pan (skillet) heat the oil and fry for 7 to 8 minutes each side.
Serves 4

Lamb and Veal Burgers

METRIC/IMPERIAL	AMERICAN
225 g/8 oz finely minced lamb	½ lb finely ground lamb
225 g/8 oz finely minced veal	½ lb finely ground veal
2 tablespoons fresh breadcrumbs	2 tablespoons soft bread crumbs
1 onion, grated	1 onion, grated
grated rind of ½ orange	grated rind of ½ orange
1 tablespoon orange juice	1 tablespoon orange juice
½ teaspoon thyme	½ teaspoon thyme
salt	salt
freshly ground black pepper	freshly ground black pepper

Combine all the ingredients in a bowl and mix well. Shape into 4 burgers. Place under a preheated grill (broiler) and cook for 6 to 7 minutes each side. Alternatively, fry the burgers in a lightly greased frying pan (skillet).
Serves 4

Index

The publishers would like to acknowledge Melvin Grey for the
photographs on pages 6 and 35. Illustrations by Lindsay Blow

PDO 83-1258